Internet in an Hour for Students

Jennifer Frew
Don Mayo
Kathy Berkemeyer

Acknowledgements

To Don for always being a phone call away, and to Midori, who puts her heart and soul into everything she does.

Jennifer Frew

To Jen for her double-duty efforts as Major Domo of the sanity patrol, Lisa Miller for always being available to help and laugh, and Marivel for her unconditional encouragement.

Don Mayo

Dedicated to the memory of my parents, John and Gert Madden.

Kathy Berkemeyer

Managing Editor	Technical Editors	English Editors	Illustrations	Design and Layout
Jennifer Frew	Monique Peterson	Jennifer Frew	Ryan Sather	Elsa Johannesson
	Cathy Vesecky	Monique Peterson		Midori Nakamura
				Paul Wray

PL
0012.6
FAE

Contents

Internet in an Hour for Students i

Contents

Introduction

This Book is Designed for You if . . .

you are a busy high school or college student doing research on the Internet, you are about to apply to college or graduate school, or you're looking for your first job.

The Internet and especially the World Wide Web provide a vast and ever-growing resource where you can find information and research tools to help you spend your time more effectively. This book shows you where and how to find the best resources available.

This book has two main sections, Internet Basics and Web Resources.

Internet Basics

In Internet Basics, you can learn how to:

- Use Netscape Navigator to browse the World Wide.
- Send and receive e-mail messages with Netscape Messenger.
- Use Internet Explorer to browse the World Wide Web.
- Send and receive e-mail messages with Microsoft Outlook Express.
- Access the Internet using America Online.
- Send and receive e-mail messages with America Online.
- Find information on the Web with search engines.

Web Resources

Web Resources shows you ways you can use the Web to get the information you need.

Web Resources is organized by general categories (such as Finding Information, Homework Helpers and Writing and Research, Going to College, Getting a Job, News and Technology, and Coping, then by topics (such as Financing Your Education and The Internet Public Library).

Each topic showcases top Web sites that offer practical business resources. Each Web site listing provides you with the site's URL (Web address) and a brief description of how the site can help you. In many cases an illustration of the web site is also provided.

Appendices

These Appendices give you additional reference information about the following topics:

Viruses
An overview of what computers viruses can do to your computer and how to avoid them.

Emoticons and Abbreviations
Symbols and abbreviations used when communicating electronically.

Netiquette
A guide to using "net etiquette" when communicating and browsing online.

Glossary
A listing of Internet and World Wide Web terminology and definitions.

What Do I Need to Use This Book

This book assumes that you have some general knowledge and experience with computers and that you already know how to perform the following tasks:

- Use a mouse (double-click, etc.).
- Make your way around Microsoft Windows 95.
- Install and run programs.

If you are completely new to computers as well as the World Wide Web, you may want to refer to DDC's **Learning Microsoft Windows 95** or **Learning the Internet**.

This book also assumes that you have access to browser applications such as Microsoft Internet Explorer 4.0, Netscape Navigator 4.0, or America Online.

√ *If you do not currently have these applications, contact your Internet Service Provider for instructions on how to download them. You can also use other browsers or previous versions such as Explorer 3.0 and Navigator 3.0 to browse the Web.*

You must have an Internet connection, either through your school, your office, or an online service such as America Online or CompuServe. How to get connected to the Internet is not covered in this book.

Please read over the following list of "must haves" to ensure that you are ready to be connected to the Internet.

- A computer (with a recommended minimum of 16 MB of RAM) and a modem port.

- A modem (with a recommended minimum speed of 14.4kbps, and suggested speed of 28.8kbps) that is connected to an analog phone line (assuming you are not using a direct Internet connection through a school, corporation, etc.).

- Established access to the Internet through an online service, independent Internet service provider, etc.

- A great deal of patience. The Internet is a fun and exciting place. But getting connected can be frustrating at times. Expect to run into occasional glitches, to get disconnected from time to time, and to experience occasional difficulty in viewing certain Web pages or features. The more up-to-date your equipment and software are, however, the less difficulty you will probably experience.

Internet Cautions

ACCURACY: Be cautious not to believe everything on the Internet. Almost anyone can publish information on the Internet, and since there is no Internet editor or monitor, some information may be false. All information found on the World Wide Web should be checked for accuracy through additional reputable sources.

SECURITY: When sending information over the Internet, be prepared to let the world have access to it. Computer hackers can find ways to access anything that you send to anyone over the Internet, including e-mail. Be cautious when sending confidential information to anyone.

VIRUSES: These small, usually destructive computer programs hide inside of innocent-looking programs. Once a virus is executed, it attaches itself to other programs. When triggered, often by the occurrence of a date or time on the computer's internal clock/calendar, it executes a nuisance or damaging function, such as displaying a message on your screen, corrupting your files, or reformatting your hard disk.

BASICS

Netscape Navigator: 1

◆ About Netscape Navigator ◆ Start Netscape Navigator
◆ The Netscape Screen ◆ Exit Netscape Navigator

About Netscape Navigator

- Netscape Navigator 4.0 is the Internet browser component of Netscape Communicator, a set of integrated tools for browsing the World Wide Web, finding and downloading information, shopping for and purchasing goods and services, creating Web pages, and communicating with others with e-mail. This chapter focuses on the Netscape Navigator browser. Netscape Messenger, the e-mail component, is covered in Chapters 4-6.

Start Netscape Navigator

To start Netscape Navigator (Windows 95):

- Click the Start button ![Start].

- Click Programs, Netscape Communicator, Netscape Navigator.

  OR

- If you have a shortcut to Netscape Communicator ![Netscape Communicator icon] on your desktop, double-click it to start Netscape Navigator.

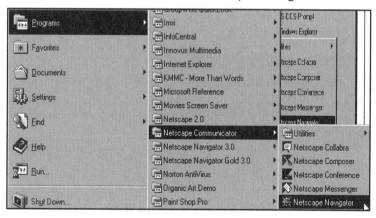

√ *The first time you start Netscape Communicator, the New Profile Setup dialog box appears. Enter information about your e-mail name and service provider in the dialog boxes that appear. If you do not know the information, you can leave it blank until you are ready to fill it in.*

2

The Netscape Screen

■ The Netscape Navigator screen contains features that will be very helpful as you explore the Internet. Some of these features are constant and some change depending on the Web site visited or the task attempted or completed.

√ *To gain more space on screen, you may want to hide toolbars and the Location line. Go to the View menu and select the desired hide/show options.*

Title bar   Displays the name of the program (Netscape) and the current Web page (Welcome to Netscape). Note the standard Windows minimize, maximize/restore, and close buttons at the right.

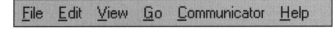

Menu bar   Displays menus, which provide drop-down lists of commands for executing Netscape tasks.

Navigation toolbar   Contains buttons for moving between and printing Web pages. The name and icon on each button identify the command for the button. You can access these commands quickly and easily by clicking the mouse on the desired button.

If the toolbar buttons are not visible, open the View menu and click Show Navigation Toolbar.

Location toolbar   Displays the electronic address of the currently displayed Web page in the Location field. You can also type the electronic address of a Web page in the Location field and press Enter to access it. A Web site address is called a Uniform Resource Locator (URL).

If the Location toolbar is not visible, open the View menu and click Show Location Toolbar.

 The Location toolbar also contains the Bookmarks QuickFile button. Click this button to view a list of sites that you have bookmarked for quick access. (For more information on bookmarks, see "Netscape Navigator: 3" on page 9.)

 The Location button is also located on this toolbar. The word *Netsite* displays if the current Web site uses Netscape software. The word *Location* replaces Netsite if the site does not use Netscape as its primary software.

Personal toolbar   Contains buttons or links that you add to connect to your favorite sites. When you install Netscape Communicator, the Internet, Lookup, New&Cool, and Netcaster buttons are on the Personal toolbar by default. You can delete these buttons and add your own by displaying the desired Web site and dragging the Location icon onto the Personal toolbar.

Netscape's status indicator   Netscape's icon pulses when Netscape is processing a request (command) that you enter. To return immediately to Netscape's home page, click on this icon.

Status bar   When a Web page is opening, the Status bar indicates progress by a percentage displayed in the center and the security level of the page being loaded by a lock in the far-left corner. When you place the cursor over a hyperlink, the Status bar displays the URL of the link.

Component toolbar   The buttons on this toolbar are links to other Communicator components: Navigator, (Messenger) Mailbox, (Collabra) Discussions, and (Page) Composer.

Exit Netscape Navigator

■ Exiting Netscape Navigator and disconnecting from your Internet Service Provider (ISP) are two separate steps. You can actually disconnect from your service provider and still have Netscape Navigator open. (Remember that you must first establish a connection to the Internet via your ISP to use Netscape to access information on the Web.) You can also disconnect from Navigator and still have your ISP open.

■ There are times when you may want to keep Netscape open to read information obtained from the Web, access information stored on your hard disk using Netscape, or to compose e-mail to send later. If you don't disconnect from your ISP and you pay an hourly rate, you will continue incurring charges.

> **CAUTION** When you exit Netscape, you do not necessarily exit from your Internet service provider. Be sure to check the disconnect procedure from your ISP so that you will not continue to be charged for time online. Most services disconnect when a certain amount of time passes with no activity.

√ *Once you disconnect from your ISP, you can no longer access new Web information. Remember: Netscape Navigator is a browser; it is not an Internet connection.*

√ *You can disconnect from your ISP and view Web information accessed during the current session using the Back and Forward toolbar buttons. This is because the visited sites are stored in the memory of your computer. However, Web sites visited during the current session are erased from your computer memory when you exit Netscape.*

Netscape Navigator: 2

◆ **The Navigation Toolbar**
◆ **URLs (Uniform Resource Locator)** ◆ **Open World Wide Web Sites**

The Navigation Toolbar

■ The Netscape Navigation toolbar displays buttons for Netscape's most commonly used commands. Note that each button contains an icon and a word describing the button's function. Choosing any of these buttons activates the indicated task immediately.

■ If the Navigation toolbar is not visible, select Show Navigation Toolbar from the View menu.

 Moves back through pages previously displayed. Back is available only if you have moved around among Web pages in the current Navigator session; otherwise, it is dimmed.

 Moves forward through pages previously displayed. Forward is available only if you have used the Back button; otherwise, it is dimmed.

 Reloads the currently displayed Web page. Use this button if the current page is taking too long to display or to update the current page with any changes that may have been made since the page was downloaded.

 Displays the home page.

 Displays Netscape's Net Search Page. You can select one of several search tools from this page.

 Displays a menu with helpful links to Internet sites that contain search tools and services.

 Prints the displayed page, topic, or article.

 Displays security information for the displayed Web page as well as information on Netscape security features.

Stops the loading of a Web page.

URLs (Uniform Resource Locator)

■ Every Web site has a unique address called its URL (Uniform Resource Locator). A URL has four parts:

Part	Example	Description
Protocol	**http://**	The protocol indicates the method used for communicating on the internet The most common is http:// , which stands for Hypertext Transfer Protocol. Another protocol—ftp:// (file transfer protocol)—is used with internet sites designed to make files available for uploading and downloading.
Address type	**www.**	www. stands for World Wide Web and indicates that the site is located on the Web. Occasionally, you may find other address types, but www. addresses are the most common.
Identifier of the site's owner	**ddcpub**	This part of the address identifies who is responsible for the Web site.
Domain	**.com, .gov, .org, .edu, etc.** (see below)	The domain indicates the kind of organization that sponsors the site (company, government, non-profit organization, educational institution, and so on).

■ For example, the DDC publishing URL breaks down as follows:

http://www.ddcpub.com

Hypertext Transfer Protocol   World Wide Web   Company name   Domain

■ There are seven common domains:

com	Commercial enterprise	**edu**	Educational institution
org	Non-commercial organization	**mil**	U. S. Military location
net	A network that has a gateway to the Internet	**gov**	Local, state, or federal government location
int	International organization		

Open World Wide Web Sites

■ There are several ways to access a Web site. If you know the site's address, you can enter the correct Web address (URL) on the Location field on the Location toolbar.

■ If the address you are entering is the address of a site you have visited recently or that you have bookmarked (see "Netscape Navigator: 3" on page 9 for more information on Bookmarks), you will notice as you begin to type the address that Netscape attempts to complete it for you. If the address that Netscape suggests is the one you want, press Enter.

■ If the address that Netscape suggests is not correct, keep typing to complete the desired address and then press Enter. Or, you can click the down arrow next to the Location field to view a list of other possible matches, select an address, and press Enter.

■ You can also enter the URL in the Open Page dialog box. To do so, select Open Page from the File menu, select Navigator, type the URL, and click Open.

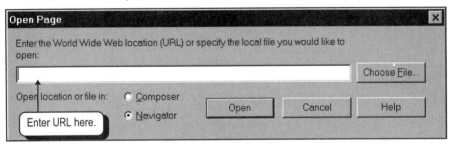

■ There are a couple of shortcuts for entering URL addresses. One shortcut involves omitting the http://www. prefix from the Web address. Netscape assumes the **http://** protocol and the **www** that indicates that the site is located on the Web. If you are trying to connect to a company Web site, entering the company name is generally sufficient. Netscape assumes the **.com** suffix. For example, entering **ddcpub** on the location line and pressing Enter would reach the **http://www.ddcpub.com** address.

√ *Don't be discouraged if the connection to the World Wide Web site is not made immediately. The site may be off-line temporarily. The site may also be very busy with others users trying to access it. Be sure the URL is typed accurately. Occasionally, it takes several tries to connect to a site.*

Netscape Navigator: 3

◆ History List ◆ Bookmarks ◆ Add Bookmarks
◆ Delete Bookmarks ◆ Print Web Pages

History List

■ While you move back and forth among Web sites, Netscape automatically records each of these site locations in a **history** list, which is temporarily stored on your computer. You can use the history list to track what sites you have already visited or to jump to a recently viewed site.

  √ *As you move from one site to another on the Web, you may find yourself asking, "How did I get here?" The History list is an easy way to see the path you followed to get to the current destination.*

■ To view the history list, click <u>H</u>istory on the <u>C</u>ommunicator menu, or press Ctrl+H. To link to a site shown in the history list, double-click on it.

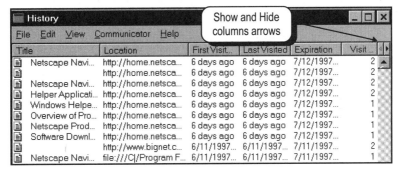

Bookmarks

■ A **bookmark** is a placeholder containing the title and URL of a Web page that, when selected, links directly to that page. If you find a Web site that you like and want to revisit, you can create a bookmark to record its location. (See "Add Bookmarks" on page 10.) The Netscape bookmark feature maintains permanent records of the Web sites in your bookmark files so that you can return to them easily.

- You can view the Bookmarks menu by selecting <u>B</u>ookmarks from the <u>C</u>ommunicator menu or by clicking on the Bookmarks QuickFile button 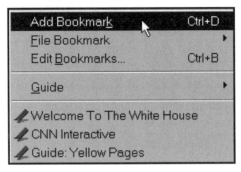 on the Location toolbar. The drop-down menu shown below appears.

Add Bookmarks

- Display the Web page to add, go to <u>B</u>ookmarks on the Communicator menu and click Add Bookmar<u>k</u>.

Netscape does not confirm that a bookmark has been added to the file.

- You can create bookmarks from addresses in the History folder. Click <u>C</u>ommunicator, <u>H</u>istory and select the listing to bookmark. Right-click on it and choose Add To Bookmar<u>k</u>s from the menu.

Delete Bookmarks

- Bookmarks may be deleted at anytime. For example, you may wish to delete a bookmark if a Web site no longer exists or remove one that is no longer of interest to you.

- To delete a bookmark do the following:
  - Click <u>C</u>ommunicator.
  - Click <u>B</u>ookmarks.
  - Click Edit <u>B</u>ookmarks.
  - In the Bookmarks window, select the bookmark you want to delete by clicking on it from the bookmark list.
  - Press the Delete key.

OR

- Right-click on the bookmark and select <u>D</u>elete Bookmark from the drop-down menu.

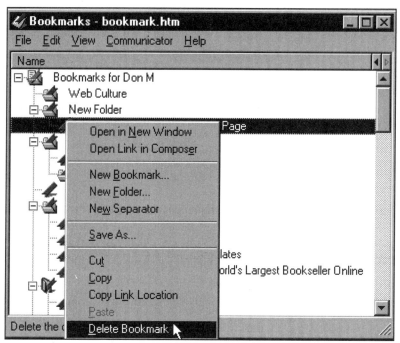

Print Web Pages

- One of the many uses of the Internet is to print out information. You can print a page as it appears on screen, or you can print it as plain text. Only displayed pages can be printed.
- To print a Web page, display it and do the following:

  - Click the Print button on the Navigation toolbar.

  OR

  - Click <u>P</u>rint on the <u>F</u>ile menu.
  - In the Print dialog box that displays, select the desired print options and click Print.
- In most cases, the Web page will be printed in the format shown in the Web page display.

◆ **Configure Netscape Mail** ◆ **Start Netscape Messenger**
◆ **The Message List Window** ◆ **Get New Mail** ◆ **Read Messages**
◆ **Delete a Message** ◆ **Print Messages** ◆ **Bookmark a Message**

Configure Netscape Mail

√ *This section assumes that you have already set up an e-mail account with a service provider. If you do not have an e-mail address, contact your Internet Service Provider. Establishing a modem connection and configuring your computer to send and receive mail can be frustrating. Don't be discouraged; what follows are steps that will get you connected, but some of the information may have to be supplied by your Internet Service Provider. Calling for help will save you time and frustration.*

■ The Netscape Communicator browser suite includes a comprehensive e-mail program called Netscape Messenger, which allows you to send, receive, save, and print e-mail messages and attachments.

■ Before you can use Messenger to send and receive e-mail, you must configure the program with your e-mail account information (user name, e-mail address, and mail server names). You may have already filled in this information if you completed the New Profile Setup Wizard when you installed Netscape Communicator.

■ You may have configured Netscape Messenger to receive and send e-mail messages when you first installed the program. If not, follow these steps to get connected. You can also use these steps to update and change settings to your e-mail account.

Identity Settings

• Open the Edit menu on the Netscape Navigator or Netscape Messenger menu and select Preferences. Click Identity in the Mail & Groups Category list to and do the following:

Enter your name and e-mail address in the first two boxes. Enter any other optional information in the Identity dialog box.

12

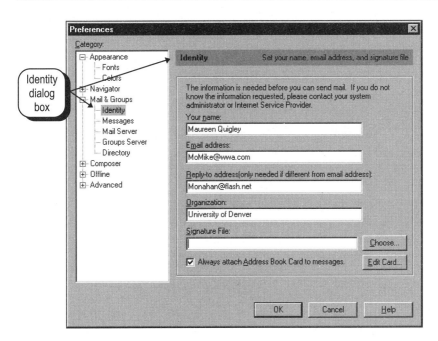

Mail Server Preference Settings

- Click Mail Server to configure your mailbox so that you can send and receive mail.

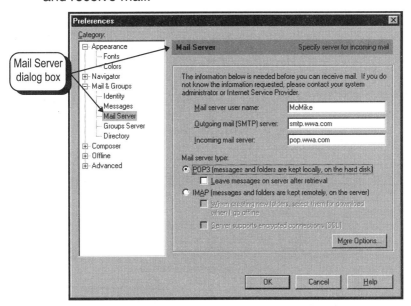

- Enter mail server user name in the first box. This is usually the part of your e-mail address that appears in front of the @ sign.

- Enter your outgoing and incoming mail server. Check with your Internet Service Provider if you are not sure what these settings are.

- Click OK to save and close the Preference settings. You should now be able to send and receive e-mail messages and/or files.

Start Netscape Messenger

■ To start Netscape Messenger:

- Click the Mailbox icon  on the Component bar.

  OR

- Start the Netscape Messenger program from the Netscape Communicator submenu on the Start menu.

The Message List Window

■ After you launch Messenger, a message list window will open, displaying the contents of the e-mail Inbox folder. You can retrieve, read, forward, and reply to messages from this window.

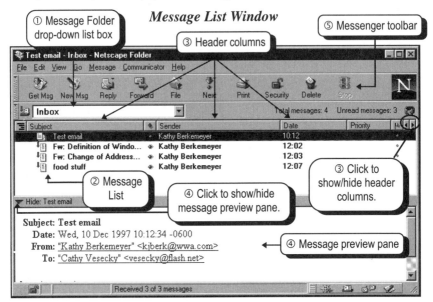

Message List Window

- The message list window includes the following:

① The **Message Folder drop-down list box** displays the currently selected message folder, the contents of which are displayed in the message list below the drop-down box. Click the down arrow to display a list of other message folders. Select a different folder from the list to display its contents in the message list area.

② The **message list** displays a header for each of the messages contained in the currently selected message folder (Inbox is the default).

③ **Header columns** list the categories of information available for each message, such as subject, sender, and date. You can customize the display of the header columns in a number of ways:

- Resize column widths by placing the mouse pointer over the right border of a column until the pointer changes to a double arrow, and then click and drag the border to the desired size.

- Rearrange the order of the columns by clicking and dragging a header to a new location in the series.

- Show/hide different columns by clicking the arrow buttons on the upper-right side of the message list window.

  √ *If text in a message header is cut off so that you cannot read it all, position the mouse pointer on the header in the column containing the cropped text. A small box will display the complete text for that column of the header, as in the example below:*

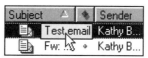

④ The **message preview pane** displays the content of the message currently selected from the message list. You can show/hide the preview pane by clicking on the blue triangle icon in the bottom-left corner of the message list pane. You can resize the preview pane or the message list pane by placing the pointer over the border between the two panes until the pointer changes to a double arrow and then dragging the border up or down to the desired size.

⑤ The **Messenger toolbar** displays buttons for activating Netscape Messenger's most commonly used commands. Note that each button contains an image and a word describing the function. Choosing any of these buttons will activate the indicated task immediately.

Messenger Toolbar Buttons and Functions

 Retrieves new mail from your Internet mail server and loads it into the Inbox message folder.

 Opens the Message Composition screen allowing you to compose new mail messages.

 Allows you to reply to the sender of an e-mail message or to the sender and all other recipients of the e-mail message.

 Forwards a message you have received to another address.

 Stores the current message in one of six Messenger default file folders or in a new folder that you create.

 Selects and displays the next of the unread messages in your Inbox.

 Prints the displayed message.

 Displays the security status of a message.

 Deletes the selected message. Deleted messages are moved to the Trash folder. You must delete contents of Trash folder to remove messages from your computer.

Get New Mail

- Since new e-mail messages are stored on a remote ISP mail server, you must be connected to the Internet to access them. To retrieve new messages to your computer, click the Get Msg button  on the Messenger toolbar.

- In the Password Entry dialog box that follows, enter your e-mail password in the blank text box and click OK. (If you do not know your e-mail password, contact your ISP.)

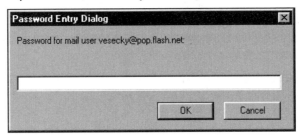

√ *Messenger saves your password for the rest of the current Messenger session. You must re-enter it each time you retrieve new mail, unless you set Messenger to save your password permanently. To do so:*

- Click Edit, Preferences.

- Click once on Mail Server under Mail & Groups.

- Click the More Options button.

- Select the Remember my mail password check box and click OK twice.

■ The Getting New Messages box opens, displaying the status of your message retrieval.

■ Once your new messages are retrieved, they are listed in the message list window. By default, Messenger stores new mail messages in the Inbox folder.

Read Messages

■ You can read a message in the preview pane of the message list window or in a separate window.

■ To read a message in the preview pane, click on the desired message header in the message list. If the message does not appear, click on the blue triangle icon at the bottom of the message list window to display the preview pane.

■ To open and read a message in a separate window, double-click on the desired message header in the message list. You can close a message after reading it by clicking File, Close or by clicking on the Close button (X) in the upper-right corner of the window.

■ To read the next unread message, click the Next button Next on the Messenger toolbar. Or, if you have reached the end of the current message, you can press the spacebar to proceed to the next unread message.

- Once you have read a message, it remains stored in the Inbox folder until you delete it or file it in another folder. (See "Delete a Message" below.)

  √ *You do not have to be online to read e-mail. You can reduce your online charges if you disconnect from your ISP after retrieving your messages and read them offline.*

  √ *Icons located to the left of message headers in the message list identify each message as either unread* ▣ *(retrieved during a previous Messenger session), new* ▣ *(and unread), or read* ▤.

Delete a Message

- To delete a message, select its header from the message list window and click the Delete button [Delete] in the Messenger toolbar.

  √ *To select more than one message to delete, click the Ctrl button while you click each message header.*

Print Messages

- In order to print a message you must first display the message in either the preview pane of the message list window or in a separate window, then:

  • Click the Print button [Print] on the Messenger toolbar.

  • In the Print dialog box that appears, select the desired print options and click OK.

Print Dialog Box

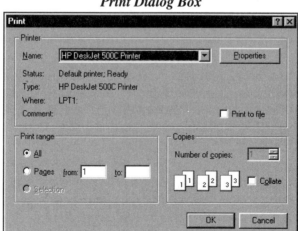

Bookmark a Message

■ You can add an e-mail message to your Bookmarks folder for easy access from anywhere within the Communicator suite. To bookmark a message:

- Display the message you want to bookmark in either the preview pane of the message list window or in a separate window.

- Select Communicator, Bookmarks, Add Bookmark.

■ Messenger will add the message to the bottom of your Bookmarks menu.

Netscape Messenger: 5

◆ Compose New Messages ◆ Send Messages
◆ The Message Composition Toolbar ◆ Reply to Mail
◆ Forward Mail ◆ Add Entries to the Personal Address Book
◆ Address a New Message Using the Personal Address Book

Compose New Messages

■ You can compose an e-mail message in Netscape Messenger while you are connected to the Internet, or while you are offline. When composing an e-mail message online, you can send the message immediately after creating it. When composing a message offline (which is considered proper Netiquette—net etiquette), you will need to store the message in your Unsent Messages folder until you are online and can send it.

■ To create a message, you first need to open Messenger's Message Composition window. To do so:

• Click the New Message button New Msg .

√ *The Message Composition window displays.*

Netscape Message Composition Window

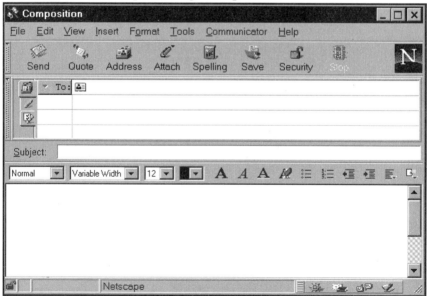

√ *You can hide any toolbar in the Message Composition screen by going to View, Hide Message Toolbar or Hide Formatting Toolbar.*

√ *If you do not know the recipient's address, you can look it up and insert it from your personal address book (see page 24) or an online directory.*

■ In the Message Composition window, type the Internet address(es) of the message recipient(s) in the To: field. Or, click the Address button [Address] on the Message Composition toolbar and select an address to insert (see pages 24-26 for more information on using the Address Book).

√ *If you are sending the message to multiple recipients, press Enter after typing each recipient's address.*

■ After inserting the address(es), click the To: icon [To:] to display a drop-down menu of other addressee options. Select any of the following options from the drop-down menu and enter the recipient information indicated.

To	The e-mail address of the person to whom the message is being sent.
CC (Carbon Copy)	The e-mail addresses of people who will receive copies of the message.
BCC (Blind Carbon Copy)	Same as CC, except these names will not appear anywhere in the message, so other recipients will not know that the person(s) listed in the BCC field received a copy.
Group	Names of newsgroups that will receive this message (similar to Mail To).
Reply To	The e-mail address where replies should be sent.
Follow-up To	Another newsgroup heading; used to identify newsgroups to which comments should be posted (similar to Reply To).

■ Click in the Subject field (or press Tab to move the cursor there) and type the subject of the message.

■ Click in the blank composition area below the Subject field and type the body of your message. Word wrap occurs automatically, and you can cut and paste quotes from other messages or text from other programs. You can also check the spelling of your message by clicking on the Spelling button  on the Message Composition toolbar and responding to the dialog prompts that follow.

Send Messages

■ Once you have created a message, you have three choices:
  • to send the message immediately
  • to store the message in the Unsent Messages folder to be sent later (File, Send Later)
  • to save the message in the Drafts folder to be finished and sent later (File, Save Draft)

To send a message immediately:

  • Click the Send button  on the Message Composition toolbar.

The Message Composition Toolbar

■ The toolbar in the Message Composition window has several features that are specific only to this screen.

■ Notice that the main toolbar buttons contain a task name and illustration.

Message Composition Toolbar

	Immediately sends current message.
	Used when replying to a message, the Quote feature allows you to include text from the original message.
	Select an address from the addresses stored in your personal address book to insert into address fields.
	By clicking the Attach button, you can send a file, a Web page, or your personal address card along with your e-mail message.
	Checks for spelling errors in the current message.

22

Lets you save your message as a draft for later use.

 Sets the security status of a message.

 Stops the display of an HTML message or a message with an HTML attachment.

- The Formatting toolbar provides commands for applying styles, fonts, font size, bulleted lists, and inserting objects.

Reply to Mail

- To reply to a message, select or open the message to reply to and

  click the Reply button .

- From the submenu that appears, select Reply to Sender to reply to the original sender only, or select Reply to Sender and All Recipients to send a reply to the sender and all other recipients of the original message. Selecting one of these options lets you reply to the message without having to enter the recipient's name or e-mail address.

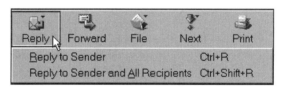

√ *The Message Composition window opens, with the To, Cc, and Subject fields filled in for you.*

- Compose your reply as you would a new message.
- To include a copy of the original message with your reply, click the

  Quote button on the Message Composition toolbar. You can edit the original message and header text as you wish.

- When you are finished, click the Send button to send the message immediately.

Forward Mail

■ To forward a message automatically without having to enter the recipient's name or e-mail address, first select or open the message to forward. Then click on the Forward button .

The Message Composition window opens, with the Subject field filled in for you.

Subject: [Fwd: Andy's Birthday Party]

■ Type the e-mail address of the new recipient in the To field, or click the Address button ▣ Address on the Message Composition toolbar and select a name from your Address Book (see "Address a New Message Using the Personal Address Book" on page 26 for information on using the Address Book).

■ If the original message does not appear in the composition area, click the Quote button ▣ Quote on the Message Composition toolbar to insert it.

■ Click in the composition area and edit the message as desired. You can also type any additional text you want to include with the forwarded message.

■ When you are done, click the Send button ▣ Send to send the message immediately. Or, select Send Later from the File menu to store the message in the Unsent Messages mailbox to be sent later. To save the reply as a draft to be edited and sent later, select Save Draft from the File menu.

Add Entries to the Personal Address Book

■ You can compile a personal address book to store e-mail addresses and other information about your most common e-mail recipients. You can then use the address book to find and automatically insert an address when creating a new message.

■ To add a name to the address book:

• Select Address Book from the Communicator menu. The Address Book window displays.

24

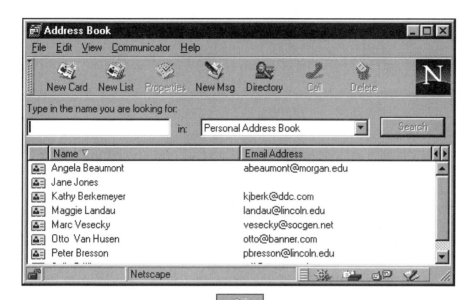

- Click the New Card button 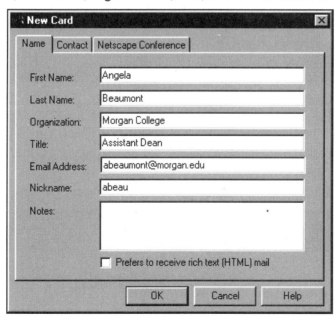 on the Address Book toolbar.
- In the New Card box that appears, enter the recipient's first name, last name, organization, title, and e-mail address.

- In the Nickname field, type a nickname for the recipient, if desired (the nickname must be unique among the entries in your address book). When addressing a message, you can use the recipient's nickname in the To field, rather than typing the entire address, and Messenger will automatically fill in the full e-mail address.

- In the Notes field, type any notes you want to store about the recipient.
- Click the Contact tab, if desired, and enter the recipient's postal address and phone number.
- Click OK.

■ You can edit an address book entry at any time by double-clicking on the person's name in the Address Book window.

■ You can automatically add the name and address of the sender of a message you are reading by selecting Add to Address Book from the Message menu and selecting Sender from the submenu. The New Card dialog box opens, with the First Name, Last Name, and E-mail Address fields filled in for you. You can enter a nickname for the person, if desired, and any other information you want in the remaining fields.

Address a New Message Using the Personal Address Book

■ To insert an address from your address book into a new message:

- Click the New Msg button New Msg to open the Message Composition window.

- Click on the Address button Address on the Message Composition toolbar and select a recipient(s) from the list in the Address Book window. Drag the selected name(s) into the To field in the Message Composition window. Click the Close button ☒ in the Address Book window when you are finished.

   OR

- Begin typing the name or nickname of the recipient in the To field of the Message Composition window. If the name is included in the Address Book, Messenger will recognize it and finish entering the name and address for you.

Netscape Messenger: 6

◆ Attached Files ◆ View File Attachments
◆ Save Attached Files ◆ Attach Files to Messages

Attached Files

- Sometimes an e-mail message will come with a separate file(s) attached. Messages containing attachments are indicated when you display a message and it contains a paperclip icon to the right of the message header. Attachment can be used, for example, when you want to send someone an Excel spreadsheet or a video clip.

- With Messenger, you can view both plain text attachments and binary attachments. **Binary** files are files containing more than plain text (i.e., images, sound clips, and formatted text, such as spreadsheets and word processor documents).

- Almost any e-mail program can read plain text files. Binary files, however, must be decoded by the receiving e-mail program before they can be displayed in readable form. This requires that the e-mail software have the capability to decode either MIME (Multi-Purpose Internet Mail Extension) or UUEncode protocol. Messenger can decode both. When a binary attachment arrives, Messenger automatically recognizes and decodes it.

View File Attachments

- File or HTML attachments are displayed in one of two ways.
  - If you select View, Attachments, Inline, you see the attachment appended to the body of the message in a separate attachment window below the message. Essentially there is a series of sequential windows—one with the message and the other with the attachment.

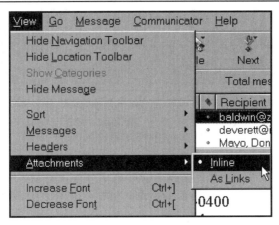

√ *Only plain text, images, and Web page attachments can be viewed inline.*

- If the attachment is HTML code, you will see a fully formatted Web page.

- If you select View, Attachments, As Links, the attachment window displays an attachment box displaying the details of the attachment. It also serves as a link to the attachment.

√ *Viewing attachments as links reduces the time it takes to open a message on screen.*

- Clicking on the blue-highlighted text in the attachment box will display the attachment.

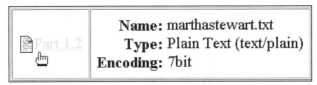

- You can right-click on the attachment icon box to display a menu of mail options such as forwarding, replying, or deleting the message.

  - By right-clicking on the actual attachment, you can choose from several file save options, such as saving the image or file in a separate file on your hard drive, as Windows wallpaper, or saving the image and putting a shortcut to the image on your desktop.

  - If you open a Web page attachment while online, you will find that the Web page serves as an actual connection to the Web site and that all links on the page are active. If you are not connected, the Web page will display fully formatted, but it will not be active.

- If an attached image displays as a link even after you select View, Attachments, Inline, it is probably because it is an image type that Messenger does not recognize. In this case, you need to install and/or open a plug-in or program with which to view the unrecognized image.

- If you know you have the appropriate application or plug-in installed, click the Save File button in the Unknown File Type dialog box and save the attachment to your hard drive or disk (see "Save Attached Files" below). Then start the necessary application or plug-in and open the saved attachment file to view it.

- If you do not have the necessary application or plug-in, click on the More Info button in the Unknown File Type dialog box. The Netscape Plug-in Finder Web page opens, displaying some general information about plug-ins, a list of plug-ins that will open the selected attachment, and hyperlinks to Web sites where you can download the given plug-ins.

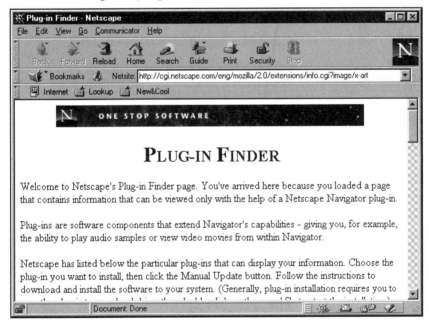

Save Attached Files

- You can save an attached file to your hard drive or disk for future use or reference. To save an attachment:

  • Open the message containing the attachment to save.

  • If the attachment is in inline view, convert it to a link (View, Attachments, As Links).

  • Right-click on the link and select Save Link As.

OR

- Click on the link to open the attachment. Select File, Save As, or, if Messenger does not recognize the attachment's file type, click the Save File button in the Unknown File Type dialog box.

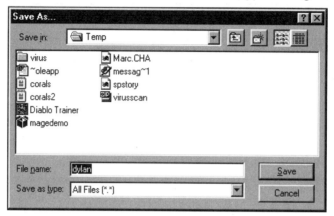

- In the Save As dialog box that follows, click the Save in drop-down list box and select the drive and folder(s) in which to save the file.
- Click in the File name text box and type a name for the file.
- Click Save.

Attach Files to Messages

- With Messenger, you can attach both plain text and binary files (images, media clips, formatted text documents, etc.) to e-mail messages. You may wish to check if your recipient's e-mail software can decode MIME or UUEncode protocols. Otherwise, binary attachments will not open and display properly on the recipient's computer.
- To attach a file to an e-mail message:

  - Click the Attach button on the Message Composition toolbar, and select File from the drop-down menu that appears.
  - In the Enter file to attach dialog box that follows, click the Look in drop-down list box and select the drive and folder containing the file to attach.
  - Then select the file to attach and click Open.

■ After you have attached a file, the Attachments field in the Mail Composition window displays the name and location of the attached file.

√ *Messages containing attachments usually take longer to send than those without attachments. When attaching very large files or multiple files, you may want to zip (compress) the files before attaching them. To do so, both you and the recipient need a file compression program, such as WinZip or PKZip.*

Attach Files and Documents

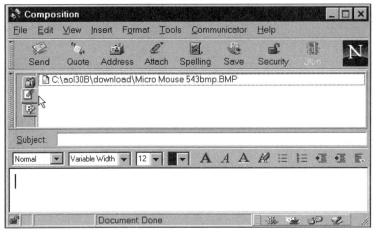

■ Once you have attached the desired files and finished composing your message, you can send the e-mail, save it in the Unsent Messages folder for later delivery, or save it as a draft for later editing.

Microsoft Internet Explorer: 7

◆ Start Internet Explorer 4
◆ Internet Explorer Screen ◆ Exit Internet Explorer

Start Internet Explorer 4

- When you first install Internet Explorer and you are using the Active Desktop, you may see the message illustrated below when you turn on your computer. If you are familiar with Explorer 3, you may want to select 1 Take a Quick Tour to learn the new features in Explorer 4. Select 2 to learn about Channels.

- To start Internet Explorer, do one of the following:

  - Click [Internet Explorer] on the Desktop.

  OR

  - Click [IE icon] on the taskbar.

  OR

  - Click the Start button [Start], then select Programs, Internet Explorer, and click Internet Explorer.

Internet Explorer Screen

■ When you connect to the World Wide Web, the first screen that displays is called a home page. The term home page can be misleading since the first page of *any* World Wide Web site is called a home page. This first page is also sometimes referred to as the start page. You could think of the home/start page as the starting point of your trip on the information highway. Just as you can get on a highway using any number of on ramps, you can get on the Internet at different starting points.

■ You can change the first page that you see when you connect to the Internet. To do this select <u>V</u>iew, Internet <u>O</u>ptions, then enter a new address in the Add<u>r</u>ess text box.

√ *The page that you see when you are connected may differ from the one illustrated below.*

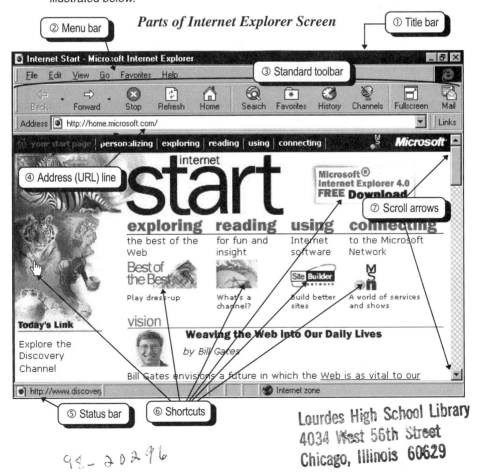

Parts of Internet Explorer Screen

② Menu bar

① Title bar

③ Standard toolbar

④ Address (URL) line

⑦ Scroll arrows

⑤ Status bar

⑥ Shortcuts

① **Title bar**   Displays the name of the program and the current Web page. You can minimize, restore, or close Explorer using the buttons on the right side of the Title bar.

② **Menu bar**   Displays menus currently available, which provide drop-down lists of commands for executing Internet Explorer tasks.

     The Internet Explorer icon on the right side of the Menu bar rotates when action is occurring or information is being processed.

③ **Standard toolbar**   Displays frequently used commands.

④ **Address (URL) line**   Displays the address of the current page. You can click here, type a new address, press Enter, and go to a new location (if it's an active Web site). You can also start a search from this line.

If you click on the arrow at the right end of the address line, you will see the links that you have visited during the current Internet session. The Links bar, containing links to various Microsoft sites is concealed on the right side of the address bar. Drag the split bar to the left or somewhere else on the screen to display current Links. If you double-click the Links button, all the current links will display. Double-click again to hide the links on the right side of the menu bar. You can add/delete links.

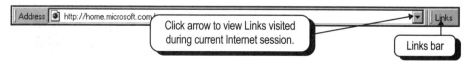

34

Links button

Buttons on Links bar

Note in the illustration above that the Links button has moved to the left side of the address bar. Just double-click on the Links button again to restore the address line. You can also drag the move bar, next to the Links button, to the left so that the Links and the Address line will both display. Drag the Links button down to display the contents of the Links bar directly below the Address bar (see illustration below).

⑤ **Status bar**   Displays information about actions occurring on the page and the Security Level. Internet Security Properties lets you control content that is downloaded on to your computer.

⑥ **Shortcuts**   Click on shortcuts (also called hyperlinks) to move to other Web sites. Shortcuts are usually easy to recognize. They can be underlined text, text of different colors, "buttons" of various sizes and shapes, or graphics. An easy way to tell if you are pointing to a shortcut is by watching the mouse pointer as it moves over the page. When it changes to a hand, you are on a shortcut. When you point to a shortcut the full name of the Web site will appear on the Status bar.

⑦ **Scroll arrows**   Scroll arrows are used to move the screen view, as in all Windows applications.

Exit Internet Explorer

■ Exiting Internet Explorer and disconnecting from your service provider are two separate steps. It is important to remember that if you close Internet Explorer (or any other browser), you must also disconnect (or hang up) from your service provider. If you don't disconnect, you'll continue incurring charges.

CAUTION *When you exit Internet Explorer, you do not necessarily exit from your Internet service provider. Be sure to check the disconnect procedure from your ISP so that you will not continue to be charged for time online. Some services automatically disconnect when a specific amount of time has passed with no activity.*

Microsoft Internet Explorer: 8

◆ **Standard Toolbar Buttons**
◆ **Open a World Wide Web Site from the Address Bar**
◆ **Open a World Wide Web Site Using the File Open Dialog Box**

Internet Explorer Toolbar

Standard Toolbar Buttons

■ The **Internet Explorer Standard toolbar** displays frequently used commands. If the Standard toolbar is *not* visible when you start Explorer, open the View menu, select Toolbars, then select Standard Buttons.

 Moves back through pages previously displayed. Back is available only if you have moved around among Web pages in the current Navigator session; otherwise, it is dimmed.

 Moves forward through pages previously displayed. Forward is available only if you have used the Back button; otherwise, it is dimmed.

 Interrupts the opening of a page that is taking too long to display. Some pages are so filled with graphics, audio, or video clips that delays can be expected.

 Reloads the current page.

 Returns you to your home page. You can change your home page to open to any Web site or a blank page (View, Internet Options, General).

 Allows you to select from a number of search services with a variety of options.

 Displays the Web sites that you have stored using the features available on the Favorites menu. Click Favorites button again to close the Favorites.

Displays links to Web sites that you have visited in previous days and weeks. You can change the number of days that sites are stored in your History folder (View, Internet Options). Click the History button again to close the History window.

 Displays the list of current channels on the Explorer bar. Click again to close the Channels window.

 Conceals Menu, titles, Status bar, and address line to make available the maximum screen space possible for viewing a Web page. Click it again to restore Menu, titles, Status bar, and address line.

 Displays a drop-down menu with various Mail and News options. You will learn about Outlook Express e-mail options in Chapters 10-12.

Open a World Wide Web Site from the Address Bar

■ Click in the Address bar and start typing the address of the Web site you want to open. If you have visited the site before, Internet Explorer will try to complete the address automatically. If it is the correct address, press Enter to go to it. If it is not the correct address, type over the suggested address that displayed on the line. To see other possible matches, click the down arrow. If you find the one you want, click on it.

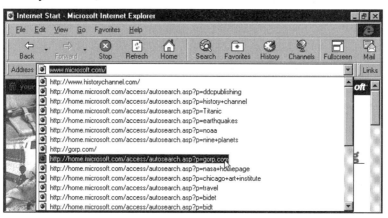

■ To turn off the AutoComplete feature, open the View menu, select Internet Options, and click the Advanced tab. Deselect Use AutoComplete in the Browsing area of the dialog box.

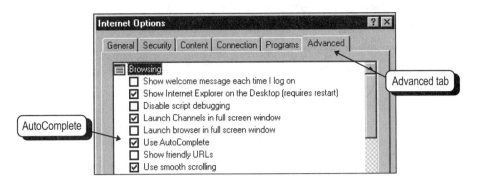

Open a World Wide Web Site Using the File Open Dialog Box

- Select File, Open, and start entering the exact address of the site you want to open. If AutoComplete is turned on and Explorer finds a potential match for the site, it will automatically appear on this line. If the match is the site you want to open, press Enter to go there. If you want to see other possible matches, click the down arrow in the open dialog box.

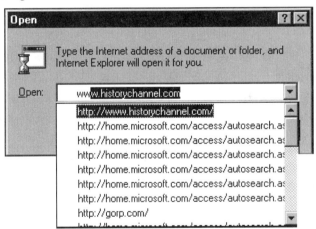

√ *Other ways of opening Web sites will be explored in this lesson. Chapters 19-21 will explain how to search for sites whose exact addresses you do not know.*

◆ **Open and Add to the Favorites Folder**
◆ **Open Web Sites from the Favorites Folder**
◆ **Create New Folders in the Favorites Folder**
◆ **AutoSearch from the Address Bar**

Open and Add to the Favorites Folder

■ As you spend more time exploring Web sites, you will find sites that you want to visit frequently. You can store shortcuts to these sites in the **Favorites folder**.

■ To add a site to the Favorites folder, first go to the desired Web site. Open the F̲avorites menu or right-click anywhere on the page and select Add To F̲avorites.

■ The following dialog box appears when you select Add to F̲avorites.

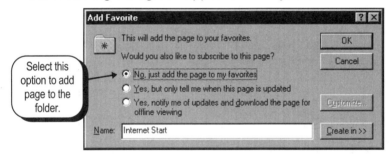

Select this option to add page to the folder.

■ The name of the Page you have opened appears in the N̲ame box. There are three ways you can store the address in response to the question "Would you also like to subscribe to this page?" Subscribing to a page means you can schedule automatic updates to that site.

• N̲o, just add the page to my favorites
Puts a shortcut to the Web site in your Favorites folder.

• Y̲es, but only tell me when this page is updated
Explorer will alert you when an update to the site is available.

• Yes, notify me of updates and d̲ownload the page for offline viewing
Explorer will automatically download and update to your computer.

■ Click OK to add the Web address to the Favorites folder.

Open Web Sites from the Favorites Folder

- Click the Favorites button [Favorites] on the Standard toolbar to open Web sites from the Favorites folder. The Explorer bar will open on the left side of the Browser window.

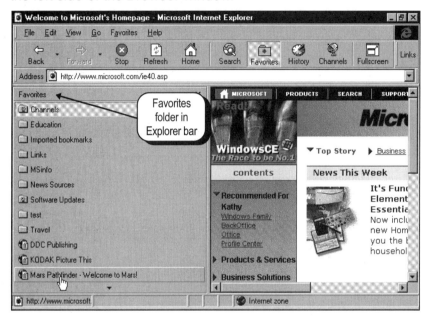

- Click on an address or open a folder and select a site. Close the Explorer bar by clicking the close button or the Favorites button on the toolbar.

- You can also open the Favorites menu and select a site from the list or from a folder.

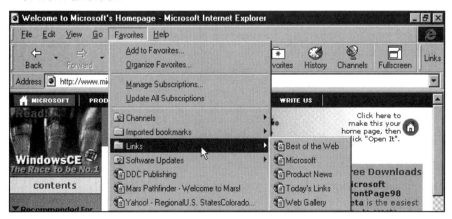

Create New Folders in the Favorites Folder

- You can create new folders before or after you have saved addresses in your Favorites folder.

  - Click Favorites and select Organize Favorites.
  - Click the Create New Folder button (shown in illustration below).

  - Type the name of the new folder and press Enter.

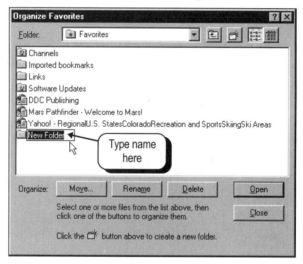

AutoSearch from the Address Bar

- In addition to displaying and entering addresses in the Address bar, you can use AutoSearch to perform a quick search directly from the Address bar.

- Click once in the Address bar and type *go, find,* or *?* and press the spacebar once. Enter the word or phrase you want to find and press Enter. For example, if you want to search for information about the year 2000, type "Find the year 2000" on the Address bar and press Enter.

- Note the Status bar displays the message "Finding site..." It is actually finding a search site. In a few moments, the results of your search displays. The keywords in your search appear in bold in the list of links that are relevant to the search string that you entered.

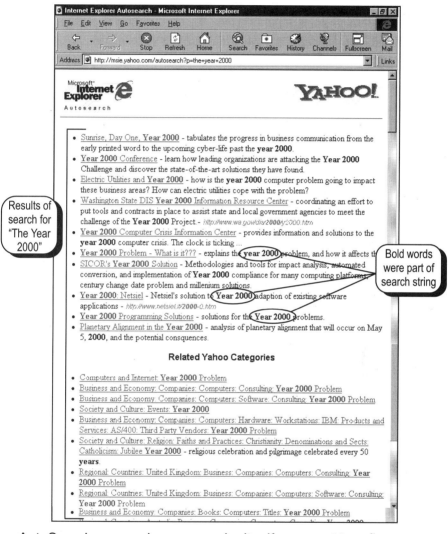

- AutoSearch uses only one search site. If you want to refine your search or see if other search engines will give you different results, click the Search button [Search] on the Standard toolbar and select a Search provider from the Choose provider drop-down list in the Explorer bar to access a different Search site.

Outlook Express: 10

◆ **Configure Outlook Express** ◆ **Start Outlook Express**
◆ **Outlook Express Main Window** ◆ **Retrieve New Messages**
◆ **The Mail Window** ◆ **Read Messages** ◆ **Delete a Message**
◆ **Print a Message** ◆ **Save a Message**

Configure Outlook Express

√ *This section assumes that you have already set up an e-mail account with a service provider. If you do not have an e-mail address, contact your Internet Service Provider. Establishing a modem connection and configuring your computer to send and receive mail can be frustrating. Don't be discouraged. What follows are steps that will get you connected, but some of the information may have to be supplied by your Internet Service Provider. Calling for help will save you time and frustration.*

■ Outlook Express is the e-mail program included in the Microsoft Internet Explorer 4.0 suite. With this program, you can send, receive, save, and print e-mail messages and attachments.

■ Before you can use Outlook Express to send and receive e-mail, you must configure the program with your e-mail account information (user name, e-mail address, and mail server names).

■ You may have already filled in this information if you completed the Internet Connection Wizard when you started Internet Explorer for the first time. If not, you can enter the information by running the Internet Connection Wizard again.

Internet Connection Wizard

• Launch Outlook Express. Open the <u>T</u>ools menu, select <u>A</u>ccounts. Click the Mail tab. Click <u>A</u>dd and select <u>M</u>ail to start the Connection Wizard.

• The Internet Connection Wizard will ask for information necessary to set up or add an e-mail account.

• Enter the name you want to appear on the "From" line in your outgoing messages. Click <u>N</u>ext.

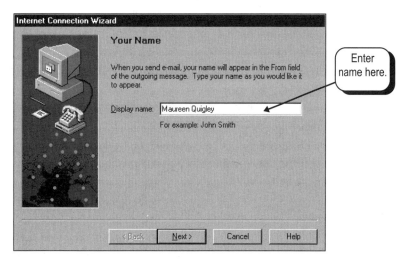

- Type your e-mail address. This is the address that people use to send mail to you. You usually get to create the first part of the address (the portion in front of the @ sign); the rest is assigned by your Internet Service Provider. Click Next.

- Enter the names of your incoming and outgoing mail servers. Check with your Internet Service Provider if you do not know what they are. Click Next.

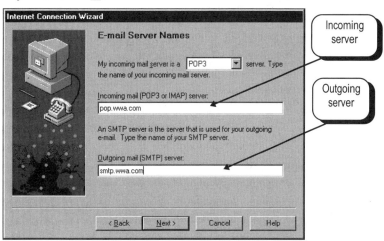

- Enter the logon name that your Internet Service Provider requires for you to access your mail. You will probably also have to enter a password. The password will appear as asterisks (******) to prevent others from knowing it. Click Next when you are finished.

- Enter the name of the account that will appear when you open the Accounts list on the Tools menu in Outlook Express. It can be any name that you choose. Click Next when you have finished.

- Select the type of connection that you are using to reach the Internet. If you are connecting through a phone line, you will need to have a dial-up connection. If you have an existing connection, click Next and select from the list of current connections.

- Select an existing dial-up connection, or select Create a new dial-up connection and follow the directions to create a new one.

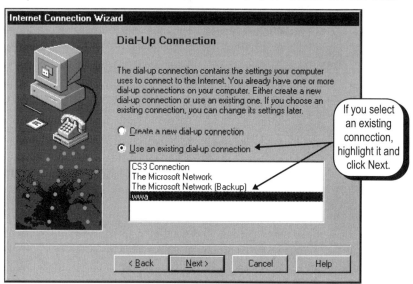

- If you select Use an existing dial-up connection you will click Finish in the last window to save the settings. You should then be able to launch Outlook Express and send and receive mail and attachments.

Start Outlook Express

■ To start Outlook Express:

- Click the Mail icon ▣ on the taskbar.

  √ *There is a chance that clicking the Mail icon from the Explorer main window will take you to the Microsoft Outlook organizational program. To use the more compact Outlook Express as your default mail program, click View, Internet Options from the Explorer main window. Click the Programs tab and choose Outlook Express from the Mail pull-down menu.*

  √ *If you downloaded Internet Explorer 4, be sure that you downloaded the standard version, which includes Outlook Express in addition to the Web browser.*

Outlook Express Main Window

■ After you launch Outlook Express, the main Outlook Express window opens by default. You can access any e-mail function from this window.

Outlook Express Main Window

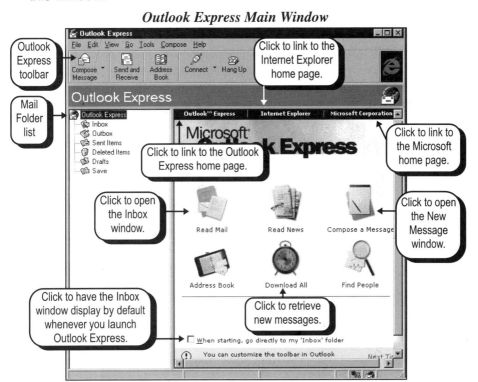

■ Descriptions of items in the main window follow below:

• The **Mail Folder list** displays in the left column of the window, with the Outlook Express main folder selected. To view the contents of a different folder, click on the desired folder in the folder list.

• **Shortcuts** to different e-mail functions are located in the center of the window. Click once on a shortcut to access the indicated task or feature.

• **Hyperlinks** to Microsoft home pages are located at the top of the window. Click once to connect to the indicated home page.

• The **Outlook Express toolbar** displays buttons for commonly used commands. Note that each button contains an image and text that describes the button function. Move your cursor over the button to display specific function information. Clicking any of these buttons will activate the indicated task immediately.

Retrieve New Messages

■ You can access the retrieve new mail command from any Outlook Express window. To do so:

• Click the Send and Receive button  on the toolbar.

■ In the Connection dialog box that displays, enter your ISP user name in the Underline User Name text box and your password in the Password text box and click OK. (If you do not know your user name or password, contact your ISP.) Outlook Express will send this information to your ISP's mail server in order to make a connection.

√ *Outlook Express will automatically save your user name and password for the rest of the current Internet session. However, you must re-enter your password each time you reconnect to the Internet or retrieve new mail, unless you set Outlook Express to save your password permanently. To do so, select the* **Save Password** *check box in the connection dialog box and click OK.*

■ Once you are connected to the Internet and Outlook Express is connected to your ISP mail server, new mail messages will begin downloading from your ISP mail server. A dialog box displays the status of the transmittal.

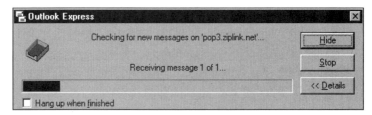

48

The Mail Window

■ After retrieving new messages, Outlook Express stores them in the Inbox folder.

■ To view your new messages, you must open the Mail window and display the contents of the Inbox folder. To do so:

• Click the Read Mail shortcut [Read Mail] in the Outlook Express main window.

■ The Mail window opens with the Inbox folder displayed. A description of the items in the Mail window appears on the following page:

Mail Window with Inbox Folder Displayed

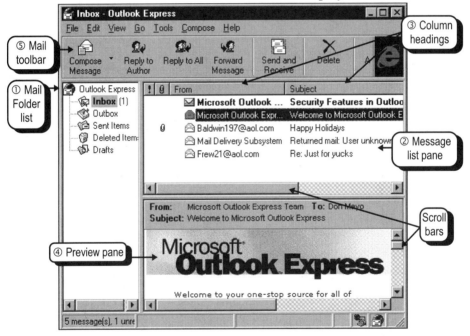

√ *In the message list, unread messages are displayed in bold text with a sealed envelope icon* ✉ *to the left of the header. Messages that have been read are listed in regular text with an open envelope icon* ✉ *to the left of the header.*

① The **Mail Folder list** displays the currently selected message folder, the contents of which are displayed in the mail list. Click on another folder to display its contents in the mail list.

② The **message list pane** displays a header for each of the messages contained in the currently selected mail folder.

③ **Column headings** list the categories of information included in each message header, such as subject, from, and date received. You can customize the display of the header columns in a number of ways:

- Resize column widths by placing the mouse pointer over the right border of a column heading until the pointer changes to a double arrow and then click and drag the border to the desired size.

- Rearrange the order of the columns by clicking and dragging a column heading to a new location in the series.

④ The **preview pane** displays the content of the message currently selected from the message list. You can show/hide the preview pane by selecting View, Layout and clicking on the Use preview pane check box. You can resize the preview pane or the message list pane by placing the pointer over the border between the two panes until the pointer changes to a double arrow and then dragging the border up or down to the desired size.

⑤ The **Mail toolbar** displays command buttons for working with messages. These commands vary depending on the message folder currently displayed (Inbox, Sent, Outbox, etc.).

Read Messages

√ *You do not have to be online to read e-mail. You can reduce your online charges if you disconnect from your ISP after retrieving your messages and read them offline.*

- You must have the Mail window open and the mail folder containing the message to read displayed.

- You can read a message in the preview pane of the Mail window, or in a separate window.

- To read a message in the preview pane, click on the desired message header in the message list. If the message does not appear, select View, Layout, Use preview pane.

- To open and read a message in a separate window, double-click on the desired message header in the message list.

  √ *The Message window opens displaying the Message toolbar and the contents of the selected message.*

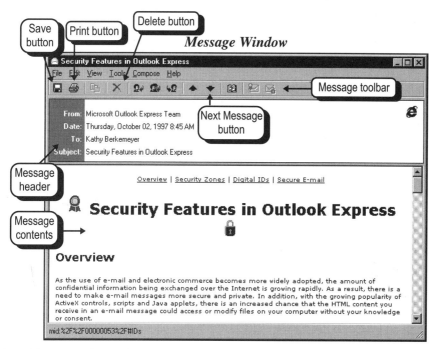

Message Window

- You can close the Message window after reading a message by clicking File, Close or by clicking on the Close button (X) in the upper-right corner of the window.

- Use the scroll bars in the Message window or the preview pane to view hidden parts of a displayed message. Or, press the down arrow key to scroll down through the message.

- To read the next unread message:
  - Select View, Next, Next Unread Message.

  OR

  - If you are viewing a message in the Message window, click the Next button ▼ on the Message toolbar.

- Once you have read a message, it remains stored in the Inbox folder until you delete it or file it in another folder. (See "Delete a Message" on the following page.)

Delete a Message

■ To delete a message:

• Select the desired header from the message list in the Mail window.

• Click the Delete button 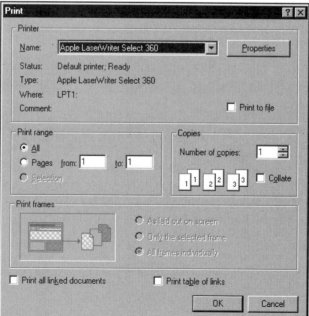 in the Mail toolbar, or select <u>E</u>dit, <u>D</u>elete.

OR

• Open the desired message in the Message window.

• Click the Delete button ⊠ on the Message toolbar.

√ *To select more than one message to delete, click the Ctrl button while you click each message header.*

Print a Message

■ To print a message:

• Select the message you want to print from the message list in the Mail window or open the message in the Message window.

• Select <u>P</u>rint from the <u>F</u>ile menu.

• In the Print dialog box that opens, select the desired print options and click OK.

Print Dialog Box

- You can bypass the Print dialog box and send the message to the printer using the most recently used print settings by opening the message in the Message window and clicking the Print button  on the Message toolbar.

Save a Message

- To save a message to your hard drive:
  - Open the desired message in the Message window and click the Save button on the Message toolbar.
  - In the Save Message As dialog box that opens, click the Save in drop-down list box and select the drive and folder in which to store the message file.

Save Messages As

  - Click in the File name box and enter a name for the message.
  - Click Save.

Outlook Express: 11

◆ **Compose New Messages** ◆ **Send Messages** ◆ **Reply to Mail**
◆ **Forward Mail** ◆ **Add Entries to the Personal Address Book**
◆ **Address a New Message Using the Personal Address Book**

Compose New Messages

■ You can compose an e-mail message in Outlook Express while you are connected to the Internet, or while you are offline. When composing an e-mail message online, you can send the message immediately after creating it. When composing a message offline, you will need to store the message in your Outbox folder until you are online and can send it. (See "Send Messages" on page 56.)

■ To create a message, you first·need to open the New Message window. To do so:

• Click the New Mail Message button ![button] on the toolbar in either the Mail window or the Main window.

The New Message window displays (see the next page).

√ *You can hide any toolbar in the New Message window by going to the View menu and deselecting Toolbar, Formatting Toolbar, or Status Bar.*

• In the New Message window, type the Internet address(es) of the message recipient(s) in the To field.

√ *If you type the first few characters of a name or e-mail address that is saved in your address book, Outlook Express will automatically complete it for you. (See page 60 for information on using the Address Book.)*

OR

Click the Index Card icon ![icon] in the To field or the Address Book button ![button] on the New Message toolbar and select an address to insert (see page 60 for information on using the Address Book).

√ *If you are sending the message to multiple recipients, insert a comma or semicolon between each recipient's address.*

54

New Message window

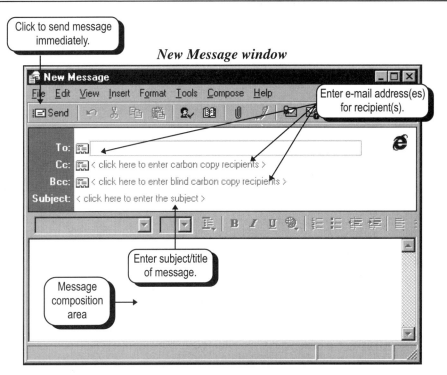

- After inserting the address(es) in the To field, you may click in either of the following fields and enter the recipient information indicated.

CC (Carbon Copy)

The e-mail addresses of people who will receive copies of the message.

BCC (Blind Carbon Copy)

Same as CC, except these names will not appear anywhere in the message, so other recipients will not know that the person(s) listed in the BCC field received a copy.

- Click in the Subject field and type the subject of the message. An entry in this field is required.

- Click in the blank composition area below the Subject field and type the body of your message. Wordwrap occurs automatically, and you can cut and paste quotes from other messages or text from other programs. You can also check the spelling of your message by selecting Spelling from the Tools menu and responding to the prompts that follow.

Send Messages

- Once you have created a message, you have three choices:
  - to send the message immediately
  - to store the message in the Outbox folder to be sent later
  - to save the message in the Drafts folder to be edited and sent later

To send a message immediately:

√ *To be able to send messages immediately, you must first select Options from the Tools menu in the Mail window. Then click on the Send tab and select the Send messages immediately check box. If this option is not selected, clicking the Send button will not send a message immediately, but will send the message to your Outbox until you perform the Send and Receive task.*

- Click the send button 📧 Send on the New Message toolbar.

  OR

  Click File, Send Message.

- Outlook Express then connects to your ISP's mail server and sends out the new message. If the connection to the mail server is successful, the sending mail icon displays in the lower-right corner of the status bar until the transmittal is complete:

- Sometimes, however, Outlook Express cannot immediately connect to the mail server and instead has to store the new message in the Outbox for later delivery. When this happens, the sending mail icon does not appear, and the number next to your Outbox folder increases by one 📁 **Outbox** [1].

- Outlook Express does not automatically reattempt to send a message after a failed connection. Instead, you need to manually send the message from the Outbox (see "To send messages from your Outbox folder" on page 57).

To store a message in your Outbox folder for later delivery:

- Select File, Send Later in the New Message window.

- The Send Mail prompt displays, telling you that the message will be stored in our Outbox folder.

- Click OK.

- The message is saved in the Outbox.

To send messages from your Outbox folder:

- Click on the Send and Receive button 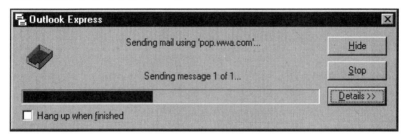 on the toolbar.

  OR

- Click <u>T</u>ools, <u>S</u>end and Receive, All Accounts.

√ *When you use the Send and Receive command, Outlook Express sends out **all** messages stored in the Outbox and automatically downloads any new mail messages from the mail server.*

- After you click Send and Receive, a dialog box opens, displaying the status of the transmittal.

To save a message to your Drafts folder:

- Click <u>F</u>ile, <u>S</u>ave.
- The Saved Message prompt displays. Click OK.

To edit and send message drafts:

- In the Mail window, click in the Drafts folder ![Drafts (1)] from the Mail Folder list.
- Double-click on the desired message header from the message list.
- In the New Message window that appears, edit your message as necessary. When you are finished, select <u>F</u>ile, S<u>e</u>nd Message to

send the message immediately, or File, Send Later to store it in the Outbox folder for later delivery.

■ Outlook Express automatically saves all sent messages in the Sent Items folder. To view a list of the messages you have sent, select the Sent Items folder [🗁 Sent Items] from the Mail Folder list. The contents will display in the message list pane.

Reply to Mail

■ In Outlook Express, you can reply to a message automatically, without having to enter the recipient's name or e-mail address.

■ When replying, you have a choice of replying to the author and all recipients of the original message or to the author only.

■ To reply to the author and all recipients:

 • Select the message you want to reply to from the message list in the Mail window.

 • Click the Reply to All button [Reply to All] on the Mail toolbar.
   OR
 • Right-click on the selected message and select Reply to All.

■ To reply to the author only:

 • Click the Reply to Author button [Reply to Author] on the Mail toolbar.
   OR
 • Right-click on the selected message and select Reply to Author.

■ Once you have selected a reply command, the New Message window opens with the address fields and the Subject filled in for you.

   √ *You can access all of the mail send commands by right-clicking on the message in the Message list.*

58

- The original message is automatically included in the body of your response. To turn off this default insertion, select Options from the Tools menu, click on the Send tab, deselect the Include message in reply check box, and click OK.

- To compose your reply, click in the composition area and type your text as you would in a new message.

- When you are done, click the Send button ⌐Send on the New Message toolbar to send the message immediately. Or, select Send Later from the File menu to store the message in the Outbox folder for later delivery. To save the reply as a draft to be edited and sent later, select Save from the File menu.

Forward Mail

- To forward a message automatically without having to enter the message subject:

  - Select the message to forward from the message list in the Mail window.

  - Click the Forward Message button on the Mail toolbar.

    The New Message window opens with the original message displayed and the Subject field filled in for you.

- Fill in the e-mail address information by either typing each address or selecting the recipients from your address book. (See "Address a New Message Using the Personal Address Book" on page 62.)

  √ *If you are forwarding the message to multiple recipients, insert a comma or semicolon between each recipient's address.*

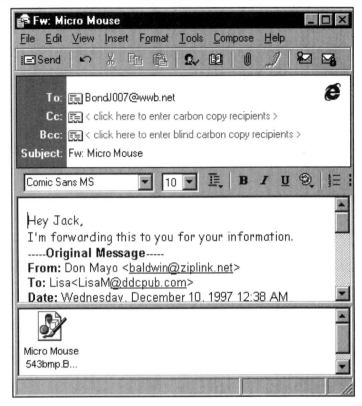

- Click in the composition area and type any text you wish to send with the forwarded message.

- When you are done, click the Send button ▣Send on the New Message toolbar to send the message immediately. Or, select Send Later from the File menu to store the message in the Outbox folder for later delivery. To save the reply as a draft to be edited and sent later, select Save from the File menu.

Add Entries to the Personal Address Book

- In Outlook Express, you can use the Windows Address Book to store e-mail addresses and other information about your most common e-mail recipients. You can then use the Address Book to find and automatically insert addresses when creating new messages.

- To open the Windows Address Book:

  - Click the Address Book button on the toolbar in the Mail window or the Main window.

The Address Book window opens, displaying a list of contacts.

Address Book Window

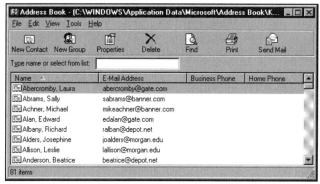

■ To add a name to the address book:

- Click the New Contact button 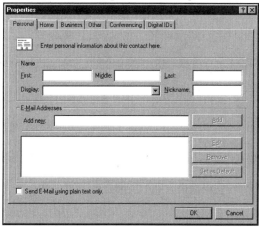 on the Address Book toolbar.

- In the Properties dialog box that displays, type the First, Middle and Last names of the new contact in the appropriate text boxes.

- Type the contact's e-mail address in the Add new text box and then click the Add button. You can repeat this procedure if you wish to list additional e-mail addresses for the contact.

- In the Nickname text box, you can enter a nickname for the contact (the nickname must be unique among the entries in your address book). When addressing a new message, you can type the nickname in the To field, rather than typing the entire address, and Outlook Express will automatically complete the address.

Contact Properties Dialog Box

- You can automatically add the name and address of the sender of a message by opening the message in the Message window, right-clicking on the sender's name in the To field, and selecting Add to Address Book from the shortcut menu.

- You can also set Outlook Express to add the address of recipients automatically when you reply to a message. To do so, select Options from the Tools menu and select the Automatically put people I reply to in my Address Book check box on the General tab.

- You can edit an Address Book entry at any time by double-clicking on the person's name in the contact list in the Address Book window.

Address a New Message Using the Personal Address Book

- To insert an address from your address book into a new message:

  - Click the Select Recipients button 📇 on the New Message toolbar.

  - In the Select Recipients dialog box that follows, select the address to insert from the contact list.

Select Recipients Dialog Box

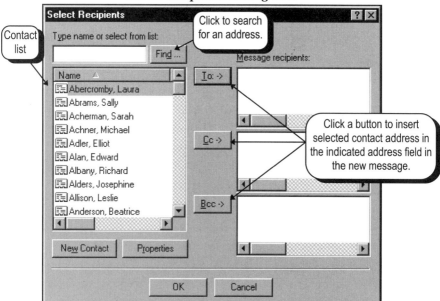

  - Click the button for the field in which you want to insert the address (To, Cc, or Bcc). Click OK to return to the New Message window when you are finished.

Outlook Express: 12

◆ **View Attached Files** ◆ **Save Attached Files** ◆ **Attach Files to a Message**

View Attached Files

- Sometimes an e-mail message will come with a separate file(s) attached. Messages containing attachments are indicated in the message list in the Mail window by a paperclip icon 🧷 to the left of the message header.

- If the selected message is displayed in the preview pane, a larger paper clip attachment icon will appear to the right of the header at the top of the preview pane.

Mail Window

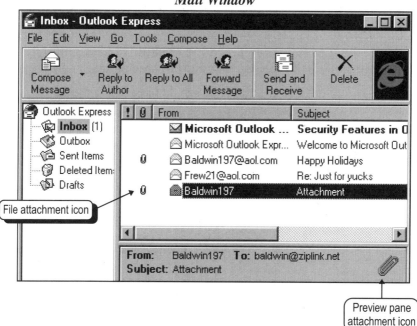

- If you open the selected message in its own window, an attachment icon will appear in a separate pane below the message.

Attachment icon

- To view an attachment:

  - Open the folder containing the desired message in the Mail window.

  - Select the message containing the desired attachment(s) from the message list to display it in the preview pane.

    If the attachment is an image, it will display in the message.

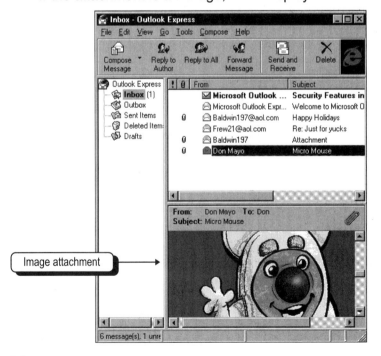

Image attachment

√ *If the image does not display, click Tools, Options, click the Read tab, select the Automatically show picture attachments in messages check box, and click OK.*

■ Other types of attachments, such as a program, word processor document, or media clip, do not display in the message, but have to be opened in a separate window. To do so:

• Click on the attachment icon 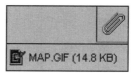 in the preview pane. A button will display with the file name and size of the attachment.

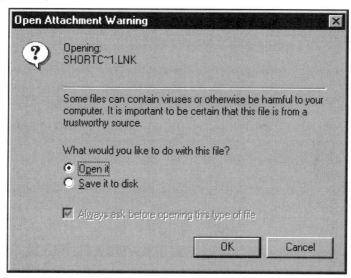

• Click on this button.

• If the Open Attachment Warning dialog box displays, select the Open it option and click OK.

■ Outlook Express will open the attached file or play the attached media clip.

■ If the attached file does not open, Outlook Express does not recognize the file type of the attached file (that is, Outlook Express does not contain the plug-in, or your computer does not contain the application needed to view it).

■ To view an unrecognized attachment, you have to install and/or open the application or plug-in needed to view it.

Save Attached Files

- If desired, you can save an attached file to your hard drive or disk for future use or reference. To save an attachment:

  - Select Save Attachments from the File menu, and select the attachment to save from the submenu that displays.

  OR

  - Right-click on the attachment icon 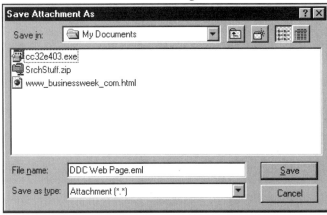 in the Message window and select the Save As option.

  - In the Save As dialog box that follows, click the Save in drop-down list box and select the drive and folder in which to save the file.

Save As Dialog Box

  - Click in the File name text box and type a name for the file.
  - Click Save.

Attach Files to a Message

■ You can attach a file to an e-mail message while composing the message in the New Message window. To add an attachment:

- Click the Attachments button 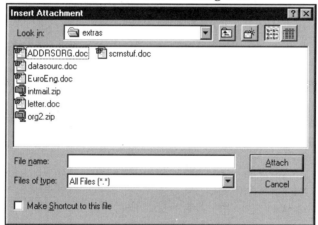 on the New Message toolbar.

  OR

- Click Insert, File Attachment.

- In the Insert Attachment dialog box that appears, click the Look in drop-down list box and select the drive and folder containing the file to attach. Then select the file and click Attach.

Insert Attachment Dialog Box

√ The attachment will appear as an icon in the body of the message.

√ Messages containing attachments usually take longer to send than those without attachments.

√ When attaching very large files or multiple files, you may want to zip (compress) the files before attaching them. To do so, both you and the recipient need a file compression program, such as WinZip or PKZip.

New Message Dialog Box

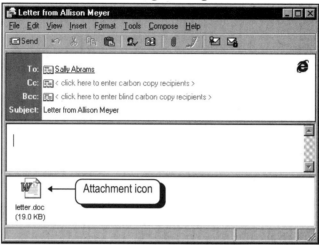

- You can also attach a file by dragging the desired file from your desktop or from Windows Explorer into the New Message window.

- You can add multiple attachments by repeating the procedure as many times as you like.

- Before you send a message containing an attachment, you may wish to make sure the recipient's e-mail program can decode the file you are sending.

America Online: 13

◆ About America Online ◆ Start America Online
◆ The AOL Home Page, Menu, and Toobar ◆ AOL Help ◆ Exit AOL

About America Online?

- America Online (AOL) is an all-purpose online service. Unlike Netscape Navigator or Microsoft Internet Explorer, AOL is not an Internet browser, yet you can browse the Internet using AOL navigation features.

- Unlike Internet browsers, AOL does not require a separate Internet Service provider for Internet access, nor does it require a separate mail server connection to access e-mail from the AOL Mail Center. When you install AOL, you configure the program to establish a dial-up connection to the AOL server using your modem. All connections to the Internet and the Mail Center are made via the AOL server.

  √ *An Internet service provider is a company that provides Internet access.*

Start America Online

- To start America Online (Windows 95):

  - Click the AOL icon on your desktop. This icon should display on your desktop after you install AOL.

  OR

  Click the Start button , Programs, America Online, America Online for Windows 95.

  - Make sure your screen name is displayed in the Select Screen Name box and type in your password in the Enter Password box.

  - Click the Sign On button to connect to the AOL server.

The AOL Home Page, Menu, and Toolbar

- After you successfully log on to America Online, you will see a series of screens. The final first screen you see is the AOL home page or start page. The AOL home page contains links to daily AOL featured areas as well as links to constant AOL areas such as *Channels* and *What's New*. You can also access your mailbox from the home page.

Home Screen Menu

File   Edit   Go To   Mail   Members   Window   Help   Sign Off

- The AOL menu displays options currently available. Click the heading to display a drop-down menu of links to AOL areas and basic filing, editing, and display options.

America Online Toolbar

- The AOL toolbar contains buttons for AOL's most commonly used commands. Choosing a button activates the indicated task immediately.

	You have new mail if the flag on the mailbox is in the up position. Click to display a list of new mail in your mailbox.
	Compose and Send Mail Messages. Displays the Composition screen for composing new mail messages.

	Channels are areas of interest arranged by category. AOLs 21 channels offer hundreds of AOL areas and Web site connections.
	New and exciting AOL areas to explore including new AOL features, areas, and special interest sites.
	People Connection takes you to the AOL chat area. Here you can access the AOL Community Center, Chat Rooms, and meet the stars in the Live chat forum.
	File Search opens the search window to the software library where you can download hundreds of software programs.
	Stocks and Portfolios links you to the latest stock market quotes, research a company or mutual fund, or find the latest financial news.
	This area not only brings you the latest headline news, weather, and sports but also allows you to search news archives by keywords. You can also see multimedia (slide show and audio) presentations of the hottest topics in the news.
	Connects you to the Web.
	Shop Online in the AOL Marketplace. Goods and services are categorized for your convenience.
	Lets you customize AOL to suit your needs. Each member area shows you step-by-step how to access and select options.
	Click to see an estimate of how long you have been online for the current session.
	Click to print whatever is displayed on your computer screen. Opens the Print dialog box where you can select from the standard print options.
	The Personal Filing Cabinet is a storage area located on your hard disk used to organize files such as downloaded e-mail messages, files, and newsgroup messages.
	Click this icon to create links or shortcuts to your favorite Web sites or AOL areas.
	This is a quick way to access the AOL member directory and to find answers to questions.
	Displays an area called Find Central. Go here to search the AOL directory using keywords and phrases.
	Each AOL area has a keyword to identify the area. Enter the Keyword for immediate access to the desired AOL area.

AOL Help

- AOL offers extensive Help so that you can learn to use AOL effectively and find answers to any questions you may have about either AOL or the Web. All AOL topics can be printed or saved to your hard disk.

- To access Help, click Help and the help topic of choice from the menu.

Exit AOL

- To exit AOL, click the close window button ☒ in the upper-right corner of the AOL screen.

  OR

  Click Sign Off, Sign Off on the menu bar.

  OR

  Click File, Exit.

America Online: 14

◆ **Access the Internet from AOL** ◆ **Open a Wold Wide Web Site**
◆ **The AOL Browser Screen** ◆ **Stop a Load or Search**

Access the Internet from AOL

■ To go to the Internet Connection:

- Click the Internet button [⊕ Internet] on the AOL main screen.

  OR

- Click **internet** from the Channels menu.

  OR

- Press Ctrl+K, type internet in the Keyword box and press Enter.
  The Internet Connection window displays.

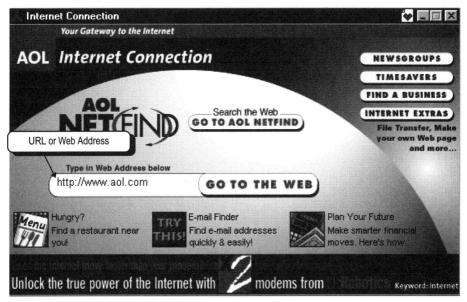

Open a World Wide Web Site

- If you know the Web address (URL), type it into the Type in Web Address below box and click the GO TO THE WEB button **GO TO THE WEB** or press Enter. If the Web address is correct, you will be connected to the Web site.

- If you wish to search the Internet, click the GO TO AOL NETFIND button **GO TO AOL NETFIND**.

The AOL Browser Screen

- Once you are connected to the Web, the screen elements change, and the Browser toolbar displays.

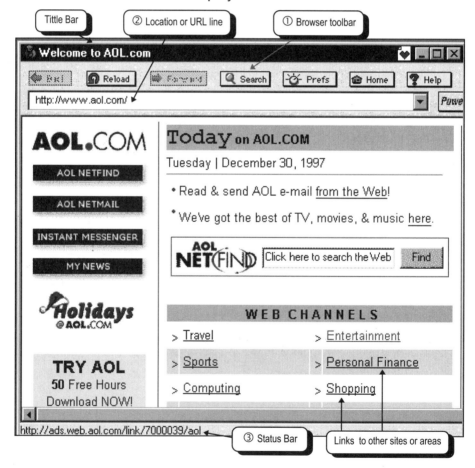

① Browser Toolbar

- The AOL Browser toolbar will help you navigate through sites you visit on the Web. Buttons on the Browser toolbar also connect you to search and Internet preference areas.

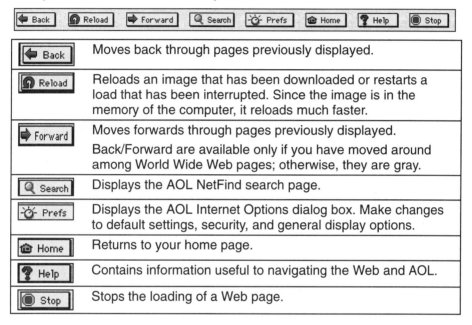

Button	Description
Back	Moves back through pages previously displayed.
Reload	Reloads an image that has been downloaded or restarts a load that has been interrupted. Since the image is in the memory of the computer, it reloads much faster.
Forward	Moves forwards through pages previously displayed. Back/Forward are available only if you have moved around among World Wide Web pages; otherwise, they are gray.
Search	Displays the AOL NetFind search page.
Prefs	Displays the AOL Internet Options dialog box. Make changes to default settings, security, and general display options.
Home	Returns to your home page.
Help	Contains information useful to navigating the Web and AOL.
Stop	Stops the loading of a Web page.

② Location Line

- AOL stores each Web address you visit during each AOL session. If you wish to return to an address you have visited during the current session, you can click the location box arrow and click the address from the pull-down list.

③ Status Bar

- The Status bar, located at the bottom of the screen, is a helpful indicator of the progress of the loading of a Web page. For example, if you are loading a Web site, you will see the byte size of the page, the percentage of the task completed, and the number of graphics and links yet to load. In many cases the time it will take to load the page will display.

Stop a Load or Search

- Searching for information or loading a Web page can be time-consuming, especially if the Web page has many graphic images, if a large number of people are trying to access the site at the same time, or if your modem and computer operate at slower speeds. If data is taking a long time to load, you may wish to stop a search or the loading of a page or large file.

- To stop a search or load:
  - Click the Stop button ⬤ Stop on the Navigation toolbar.

- If you decide to continue the load after clicking the Stop button, click the Reload button ⟳ Reload.

◆ Favorite Places ◆ Add Favorite Places ◆ View Favorite Places
◆ Delete Favorite Places ◆ AOL History List
◆ Save Web Pages ◆ Print Web Pages

Favorite Places

■ A **Favorite Place** listing is a bookmark that you create containing the title, URL, and a direct link to a Web page or AOL area that you may want to revisit. A Favorite Place listings links directly to the desired page.

■ The AOL Favorite Place feature allows you to maintain a record of Web sites in your Favorite Places file so that you can return to them easily. (See "Add Favorite Places" below.)

Add Favorite Places

■ There are several ways to mark an AOL area or Web site and save it as a Favorite Place. Once the page is displayed:

• Click the Favorite Place heart 💟 on the Web site or AOL area title bar.

🔥 TUCOWS World Wide Affiliate Site Locations! 💟 🗕🗖🗙

• Click Yes to confirm the addition of the listing.

OR

Favorite
Place icon

• Display the Web page to add, right-click anywhere on the page and select Add to Favorites from the shortcut menu.

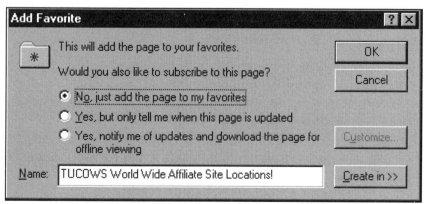

- Click the desired option from the confirmation box that displays and click OK.
- The site will automatically be added to your Favorite Places list.

View Favorite Places

■ You can view the Favorite Places file by selecting Go To, Favorite Places, or by clicking on the Favorite Places button on the AOL toolbar. Click on any listing from the list to go directly to that page.

■ The details of any Favorite Place listing can be viewed or modified by using the buttons on the Favorite Places screen.

Delete Favorite Places

■ You may wish to delete a Favorite Place if a Web site no longer exists or remove an AOL area from the listing that is no longer of interest to you.

To delete a Favorite Place:

- Click the Favorite Places button on the toolbar.
- Click on the listing to delete.
- Click the Delete button Delete from the Favorite Places screen.
  OR
- Right-click on the listing and select Delete from the pop-up menu.
  OR
- Press the Delete key.
- Click YES to confirm the deletion.

AOL History List

■ While you move back and forth within a Web site, AOL automatically records each page location. The history is only temporary and is deleted when you sign-off. AOL areas are not recorded in the history list.

■ To view the history list, click on the arrow at the end of the URL line. You can use History to jump back or forward to recently viewed pages by clicking on the page from the list.

78

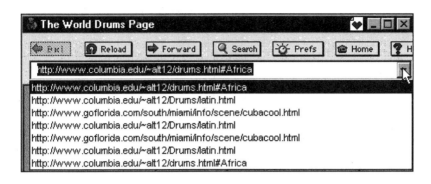

Save Web Pages

■ When you find a Web page with information that you would like to keep for future reference, or to review later offline, you can save it to your hard disk. To save a Web page:

  • Click File, Save

  • Type a filename in the File name box.

    √ *When you save a Web page, often the current page name appears in the File name box. You can use this name or type a new one.*

  • Choose the drive and folder in which to store the file from the Save in drop-down list

  • Click Save.

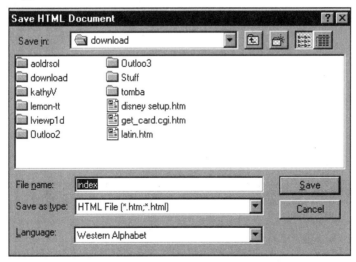

■ In most cases when you choose to save a Web page, AOL will automatically save it as an HTML file. Saving a page as an HTML file saves the original formatting and, when accessed, will display as you saw it on the Web.

- You can also save a Web page as a Plain text file which saves only the page text without the formatting or images and placeholders. You might want to do this when saving a very large file, such as a literary work or multiple-page article. To save in Plain text format, click the down arrow next to the Save as type box in the Save As dialog box and select Plain text from the list.

- You can view a saved Web page later by clicking File, Open, and entering the name and location from the Open a File box or by choosing the location and double-clicking on the file name.

Print Web Pages

- One of the many uses of the Internet is to find and print information. You can print a page as it appears on screen, or you can print it as plain text. Only displayed pages can be printed. To print a Web page, display it and do the following:

  - Click the Print button on the AOL toolbar.

  OR

  - Click Print on the File menu.

  - In the Print dialog box that displays, select the desired print options and click OK.

- In most cases, the Web page will be printed in the format shown in the Web page display.

America Online E-mail: 16

◆ Read New Mail ◆ Compose a New Mail Message
◆ Send Messages ◆ Reply to Mail
◆ Forward Mail ◆ AOL Mail Help

Read New Mail

■ There are several ways to know whether you have new mail in your mailbox: If your computer has a sound card and speakers, you will hear "You've Got Mail" when you successfully connect to AOL. The

link is replaced by the You Have Mail link, and the mailbox

icon on the main screen has the flag in the up position .

To display and read new and unread mail:

• Click the You Have Mail button on the AOL main screen.
  OR
• Click the Read New Mail button on the main screen toolbar
  OR
• Press Ctrl+R.

  √ *The New Mail list displays new and unread mail for the screen name used for this session. If you have more than one screen name, you must sign on under each name to retrieve new mail.*

  √ *New and Unread e-mail messages remain on the AOL mail server for approximately 27 days before being deleted by AOL. If you want to save a message to your hard disk, click **File, Save As** and choose a location for the message. By default the message will be saved to the Download folder.*

• To read a message, double-click on it from the New Mail list.

Compose a New Mail Message

• Click Mail, Compose Mail.
  OR
• Click the Compose Mail button on the main screen toolbar.
  OR
• Click Ctrl+M.

The Compose Mail screen displays.

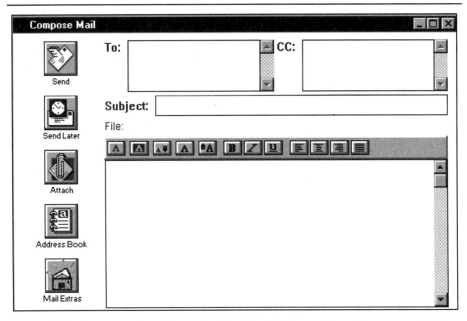

- Fill in the e-mail address(es) in the To box of the Compose Mail screen.

  OR

- Select Address Book and double-click to select an address. (See "America Online E-mail: 18" on page 88 for more information on your Address book.)

- If you are sending the same message to multiple recipients, fill in the CC: (Carbon Copy) box with the e-mail addresses of recipients who will receive a copy of this message. These names will display to all recipients of the message.

- If you want to send BCC: (Blind courtesy copies—copies of a message sent to others but whose names are not visible to the main or other recipients), put the address in parenthesis, for example: (ddcpub.com).

  √ *Multiple addresses must be separated with a comma.*

- Fill in the Subject box with a one-line summary of your message. AOL will not deliver a message without a subject heading. This is the first thing the recipient sees in the list of new mail when your message is delivered.

- Fill in the body of the message.

Send Messages

- Click the Send button to send the message immediately. *You must be online.*

  OR

- Click the Send Later button to send a message later that you have composed offline.

Reply to Mail

- You can reply to mail messages while online or compose replies to e-mail offline to send later.

- To reply to e-mail:

  - Click the Reply button from the displayed message screen. If the message has been sent to more than one person, you can send your response to each recipient of the message by

    clicking the Reply to All button. The addresses of the sender and, if desired, all recipients will be automatically inserted into the address fields.

    √ *To include part or all of the original message in your Reply, select the contents of the original message to be included in quotes in your message and click the Reply button to begin your reply.*

  - Click the Send button if you are online and want to send

    the reply immediately or click the Send Later button.

Forward Mail

■ There are times when you may want to send mail sent to you on to someone else.

■ To forward e-mail:

• Click the Forward button ⌐Forward⌐ from the displayed message screen and fill in the address(es) of the recipients of the forwarded message. The Subject heading from the original message is automatically inserted into the subject heading box.

• Click the Send button ⌐Send⌐ if you are online and want to send

the reply immediately or click the Send Later button ⌐Send Later⌐.

AOL Mail Help

■ For answers to many of your basic e-mail questions, click Mail, Mail

Center, and click on the Let's Get Started button .

◆ **Add Attachments to a Message**
◆ **Download File Attachments**

Add Attachments to a Message

■ You can attach a file to send along with any e-mail message. Before you send a file attachment—especially if it is a multimedia file—it is a good idea to make sure that the recipient's e-mail program can read the attachment. For example, files sent in MIME format cannot be viewed by AOL e-mail and require separate software to be opened.

To attach files to a message:

• Compose the message to be sent. (See "Compose a New Mail Message" on page 81.)

• Click the Attach button [Attach] on the Compose Message screen.

• Select the drive and folder where the file you wish to attach is located.

• Double-click the file to attach from the Attach File dialog box.

   √ *The attachment will appear below the Subject box.*

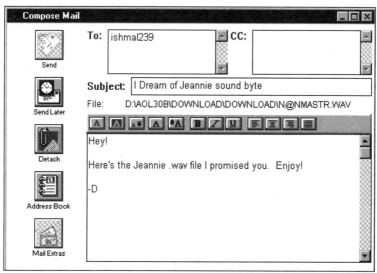

- If you are online, click the Send button [Send] to send the
message immediately, or click the Send Later button [Send Later] to
store the message in your Outgoing Mail if you are working
offline.

  √ *Multiple files must be grouped together in a single archive using a file
  compression program such as PKZIP or WINZIP. Both you and the recipient
  will need a file compression program.*

Download E-mail File Attachments

- An e-mail message that arrives with a file attachment is displayed in
  your new mail list with a small diskette under the message icon.

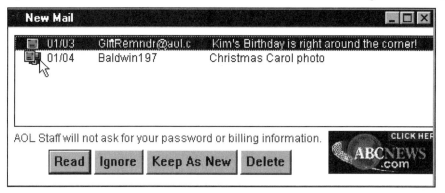

- Opening the message and viewing the attachment are two separate
  steps:

  - Open the message by double-clicking on it from the New Mail list
    (see "To display and read new and unread mail" on page 81).
    The message will display.

  - You can choose to download the file attachment immediately by
    clicking the Download File button [Download File] at the bottom of
    the displayed message screen. Click the Save button [Save]
    on the Download Manager screen to save the file, by default, to
    the AOL30/Download folder. If you desire, you can change the
    save destination folder.

86

- A status box will display while the attachment is being downloaded or transferred to your computer.

- At the end of the download, the file transfer box will close and you will see the message "File's Done."

OR

- You may choose to download the file later. Click the Download Later button **Download Later** to store the message in the Download Manager. When you are ready to download the file, click File, Download Manager, and then select the file to download. You must be online.

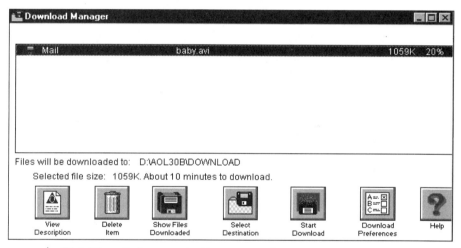

√ *Click Sign off after transfer if you want AOL to automatically disconnect when the transfer is complete.*

To change the default location of where files are stored:

- Click the Select Destination button from the Download Manager screen and choose the desired destination from the Select Path dialog box.

◆ **Add Entries to the Address Book**
◆ **Enter an Address Using the Address Book**

Add Entries to the Address Book

■ Once you start sending e-mail, you may be surprised at how many people you start to communicate with online. An easy way to keep track of e-mail addresses is to enter them into the Address Book. Once an e-mail address entry has been created, you can automatically insert it from the Address Book into the address fields.

To create Address Book entries:

• Click <u>M</u>ail, Edit <u>A</u>ddress Book. The Address Book dialog box displays.

• Click the Create button [Create] to open the Address Group box.

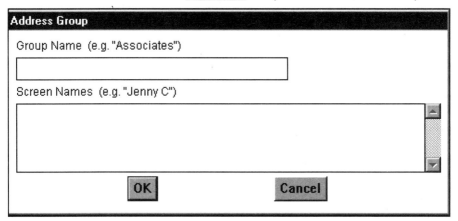

• Enter the real name or nickname of the e-mail recipient (e.g., JohnV) or the name of a Group listing (e.g., Book Club) in the Group Name box. The name you enter in this box is the name that will appear in the Address Book list.

• Press the Tab key to move to the Screen Names box and enter the complete e-mail address of the recipient or the e-mail addresses of everyone in the group listing. When entering multiple addresses such as in a group listing, each address must be separated by a comma (e.g., Baldwin168, BubbaB@ziplink.net, etc.).

- Click OK.

  √ *When sending mail to AOL members through AOL, you do not need to enter the @aol.com domain information. Enter only their screen name as the e-mail address. For all other Address Book entries you must enter the entire address.*

Delete an Address Book Entry

- Click <u>M</u>ail, Edit <u>A</u>ddress Book to open the Address Book.
- Click the name to delete.
- Click the Delete button   Delete   .
- Click Yes.
- Click OK to close the Address Book.

Enter an Address Using the Address Book

- Place the cursor in the desired address field.

- Click the Address Book button Address Book to open the Address Book.
- Double-click the name or names from the Address Book list to insert in the TO: or CC: address box and click OK.

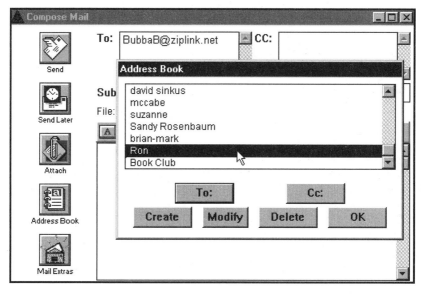

◆ Searching vs. Surfing ◆ Search Sites ◆ Search Basics

Searching vs. Surfing

- The Web is a vast source of information, but to find information that you want, you must be able to locate it. The Web has many thousands of locations, containing hundreds of thousands of pages of information.

- Unlike libraries that use either the Library of Congress or Dewey Decimal system to catalog information, the Internet has no uniform way of tracking and indexing information. You can find lots of information on the Internet; the trick is to find information that you want. Initially, it may seem easy to find information on the Web— you just connect to a relevant site and then start clicking on links to related sites. Illustrated below is an example of a search that starts out on one topic and ends on an unrelated one.

Both the Pathfinder lander and rover have stereo imaging systems. The rover, additionally, carries an alpha proton x-ray spectrometer with which it will examine the composition of the rocks. The imaging system will reveal the mineralogy of surface materials as well as the geologic processes and surface-atmosphere interactions that created and modified the surface. The instrument package will also enable scientists to determine dust particle size and water vapor abundance in the atmosphere.

- Mars Pathfinder Page - information on the mission, Mars, and other resources
- Mars global view showing the Viking and Mars Pathfinder landing sites
- Mars Mileage Guide - distance between Pathfinder and Viking landing sites and other martian features
- Mars Pathfinder Entry Strategy - the plans for Mars Pathfinder atmospheric entry and landing
- NSSDC Planetary Page

Questions and comments about this page should be addressed to:
Dr. David R. Williams, dwilliam@nssdc.gsfc.nasa.gov, (301) 286-1258
NSSDC, Mail Code 633, NASA/Goddard Space Flight Center, Greenbelt, MD 20771

NSSDC National Space Science Data Center

This Web site contains links to sites about the Mars Pathfinder mission. Click on the link to the National Space Science Data Center.

What's New in Planetary Science

Results of the Mars Pathfinder mission, including a mission summary and APXS Mars surface composition results have been published in *Science* magazine.

- The Mars Global Surveyor resumed its aerobraking activities on November 7th following an analysis of the condition of the solar panels by the project. More detail is available in the NASA press release from the press conference held on 10 November.

- The first 14 volumes of the Clementine Lunar Digital Image Model CD-ROMs are now available from NSSDC. These volumes are regional mosaics created from Clementine images showing the Moon at a resolution of 100 meters/pixel. Volume 15 has lower resolution global views and is expected at the end of 1997.

- Upcoming Planetary Events and Missions
- New and Incoming Planetary Data at NSSDC
- New and Updated Planetary Pages

This Web site contains links to sites that have broader information about space exploration. Click on the link to Upcoming Planetary Events and Missions.

Upcoming Planetary Events and Missions

Upcoming Planetary Launches and Events

1997 December 16 - <u>Galileo</u> - Europa closest flyby

1998 January 6 - <u>Lunar Prospector</u> - Launch of NASA Global Orbiter Mission to the Moon
1998 January 23 - <u>NEAR</u> - Earth Flyby
1998 April 26 - <u>Cassini</u> - Venus-1 Flyby
1998 July - <u>New Millenium Deep Space-1</u> - Launch of NASA Flyby Mission to Asteroid 3352 McAuliffe and Comet P/West-Kohoutek-Ikemura
1998 August 6 - <u>Planet-B</u> - Launch of ISAS (Japan) Orbiter Mission to Mars
1998 December - <u>Mars Surveyor '98 Orbiter</u> - Launch of NASA Orbiter Mission to Mars

> Click on Cassini link to go to a Web site that deals with a project to explore Saturn.

Cassini

Cassini has launched!

Launch Date/Time: 15 October 1997 at 08:43 UTC
Launch Vehicle: Titan IV-Centaur
Planned on-orbit mass: 2175 Kg
Power System: Radioisotope Thermal Generators (RTGs) of 630 W

The Cassini Orbiter's mission consists of delivering a probe (called <u>Huygens</u>, provided by ESA) to Titan, and then remaining in orbit around Saturn for detailed studies of the planet and its rings and satellites. The principal objectives are to: (1) determine the three-dimensional structure and dynamical behavior of the rings; (2) determine the composition of the satellite surfaces and

- This is the stream of consciousness method of searching the Internet (**surfing**). It may be interesting and fun to locate information this way, but there are drawbacks. Surfing randomly for information is time consuming and the results are frequently inconsistent and incomplete. It can also be expensive if you are charged fees for connect time to your Internet Service Provider.

- If you want a more systematic and organized way of looking for information, you can connect to one of several search sites that use **search engines** to track, catalog, and index information on the Internet.

Search Sites

- A **search site** builds its catalog using a search engine. A search engine is a software program that goes out on the Web, seeking Web sites, and cataloging them, usually by downloading their home pages.

- Search sites are classified by the way they gather Web site information. All search sites use a search engine in one way or another to gather information. Below is an explanation of how the major search services assemble and index information.

Search Engines

- A search site builds its catalog using a **search engine**. A search engine is a software program that goes out on the Web, seeking Web sites, and cataloging them, usually by downloading their home pages.

- Search engines are sometimes called **spiders** or **crawlers** because they crawl the Web.

- Search engines constantly visit sites on the Web to create catalogs of Web pages and keep them up to date.

- Major search engines include: **AltaVista**, **HotBot**, **Open Text**.

Directories

- Search **directories** catalog information by building hierarchical indexes. Since humans assemble the catalogs, information is often more relevant than the indexes that are assembled by Web crawlers. Directories may be better organized than search engine sites, but they will not be as complete or up-to-date as search engines that constantly check for new material on the Internet.

- **Yahoo**, the oldest search service on the World Wide Web, is the best example of Internet search directories. Other major search directories are: **Infoseek**, **Magellan**, **Lycos**.

Multi-Threaded Search Engines

- Another type of search engine, called a **multi-threaded** search engine, searches other Web search sites and gathers the results of these searches for your use.

- Because they search the catalogs of other search sites, multi-threaded search sites do not maintain their own catalogs. These search sites provide more search options than subject-and-keyword search sites, and they typically return more specific information with further precision. However, multi-threaded search sites are much slower to return search results than subject-and-keyword search sites.

- Multi-threaded search sites include **SavvySearch** and **Internet Sleuth**.

- If you are using Internet Explorer or Netscape Navigator, you can click on the Search button on the toolbar to access a number of search services.

92

Search Basics

- When you connect to a search site, the home page has a text box for typing the words you want to use in your search. These words are called a **text string**. The text string may be a single word or phrase, or it may be a complex string which uses **operators** to modify the search (see "Search Engines: 21" for more information on operators). Illustrated below is the opening page of Yahoo, one of the oldest and most popular search directories.

Click to initiate search.

Links to Yahoo categories

Access options to refine search.

Yahoo! Mail
free email

Shop and Win @ NetBuyer

Win a Sports Dream Trip

Search | options

Yellow Pages - People Search - Maps - Classifieds - Personals - Chat - **Email**
Holiday Shopping - My Yahoo! - News - Sports - Weather - Stoc

- **Arts and Humanities**
  Architecture, Photography, Literature...

- **Business and Economy** [Xtra!]
  Companies, Finance, Employment...

- **Computers and Internet** [Xtra!]
  Internet, WWW, Software, Multimedia...

- **Education**
  Universities, K-12, College Entrance...

- **Entertainment** [Xtra!]
  Cool Links, Movies, Music, Humor...

- **Government**
  Military, Politics [Xtra!], Law, Taxes...

- **Health** [Xtra!]
  Medicine, Drugs, Diseases, Fitness...

- **News and Media** [
  Current Events, Magazines, TV, Newspapers...

- **Recreation and Sports** [Xtra!]
  Sports, Games, Travel, Autos, Outdoors...

- **Reference**
  Libraries, Dictionaries, Phone Numbers...

- **Regional**
  Countries, Regions, U.S. States...

- **Science**
  CS, Biology, Astronomy, Engineering...

- **Social Science**
  Anthropology, Sociology, Economics...

- **Society and Culture**
  People, Environment, Religion...

Regional links

Yahooligans! for Kids - Beatrice's Guide - MTV/Yahoo! unfURLed - Yahoo! Internet Life
What's New - Weekly Picks - Today's Web Events
Visa Shopping Guide - Yahoo! Store

World Yahoos Australia & NZ - Canada - Denmark - France - Germany - Japan - Korea
Norway - SE Asia - Sweden - UK & Ireland
Yahoo! Metros Atlanta - Austin - Boston - Chicago - Dallas / Fort Worth - Los Angeles
Get Local Miami - Minneapolis / St. Paul - New York - S.F. Bay - Seattle - Wash D.C.

Smart Shopping with VISA

How to Suggest a Site - Company Info - Openings at Yahoo! - Contributors - Yahoo! to Go

- Once you have entered a text string, initiate the search by either pressing the Enter key or by clicking on the search button. This button may be called Search, Go Get It, Seek Now, Find, or something similar.

- For the best search results:
  - Always check for misspelled words and typing errors.
  - Use descriptive words and phrases.
  - Use synonyms and variations of words.
  - Find and follow the instructions that the search site suggests for constructing a good search.
  - Eliminate unnecessary words (the, a, an, etc.) from the search string. Concentrate on key words and phrases.
  - Test your search string on several different search sites. Search results from different sites can vary greatly.
  - Explore some of the sites that appear on your initial search and locate terms that would help you refine your search string.

Search Engines: 20

◆ Simple Searches ◆ Refine a Search ◆ Get Help

Simple Searches

■ Searches can be simple or complex, depending on how you design the search string in the text box.

■ A **simple search** uses a text string, usually one or two key words, to search for matches in a search engine's catalog. A simple search is the broadest kind of search.

  • The key words may be specific, such as Internet Explorer browser, current stock quotes, or Macintosh computers, or they may be general, such as software, economy, or computer.

  • The catalog search will return a list, typically quite large, of Web pages and URLs whose descriptions contain the text string you want to find. Frequently these searches will yield results with completely unrelated items.

■ When you start a search, the Web site searches its catalog for occurrences of your text string. (Some search sites don't have their own catalog, so they search the catalogs of other search sites.) The results of the search, typically a list of Web sites whose descriptions have words that match your text string are displayed in the window of your browser.

■ Each search site has its own criteria for rating the matches of a catalog search and setting the order in which they are displayed.

■ The catalog usually searches for matches of the text string in the URLs of Web sites. It also searches for key words, phrases, and meta-tags (key words that are part of the Web page, but are not displayed in a browser) in the cataloged Web pages.

■ The information displayed on the results page will vary, depending on the search and display options selected and the search site you are using. The most likely matches for your text string appear first in the results list, followed by other likely matches on successive pages.

  √ *There may be thousands of matches that contain the search string you specified. The matches are displayed a page at a time. You can view the next page by clicking on the "next page" link provided at the bottom of each search results page.*

- For example, if you do a search on the word *Greek*, you'll get results, as illustrated below, that display links to a wide range of links that have something to do with Greek. Note the number of documents that contain the search word.

√ *These examples use AltaVista to perform the search. Your results may vary with other search tools.*

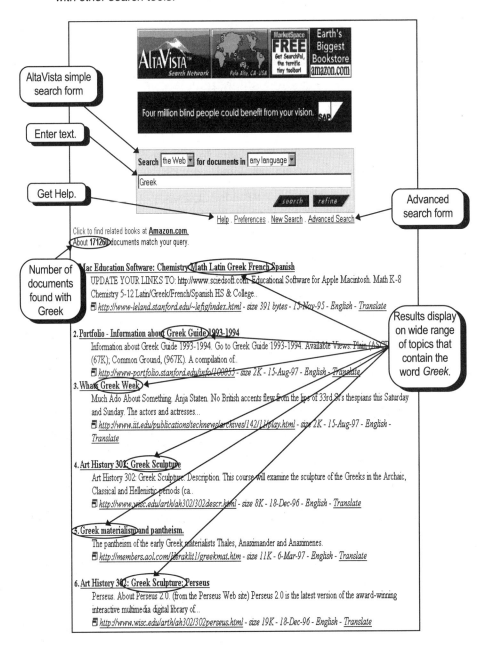

AltaVista simple search form

Enter text.

Get Help.

Advanced search form

Number of documents found with Greek

Results display on wide range of topics that contain the word *Greek*.

- You can scan the displayed results to see if a site contains the information you are looking for. Site names are clickable links. After visiting a site, you can return to the search site by clicking the Back button on your browser. You can then choose a different site to visit or perform another search.

Refine a Search

- Suppose that you only want to view links that deal with Greek *tragedies*. The natural inclination would be to enter Greek tragedies in the search string to reduce the number of documents that the search tool finds. Note, however, the number of documents that were found when Greek tragedies was entered in this search. Since the search string didn't include a special operator to tell the search engine to look for sites that contain both Greek *and* tragedies, the results display sites that contain Greek *OR* tragedies in addition to sites that contain Greek *AND* tragedies.

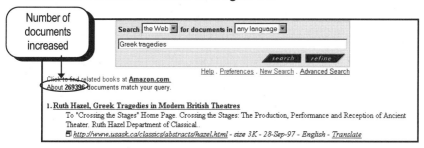

- To reduce the number of documents in this search, enter *Greek* press space once, then enter a plus sign (+) and the word tragedies (Greek +tragedies) then click Search. This tells AltaVista to look for articles that contain Greek *and* tragedies in the documents. Note the results that display when the plus is added to the search.

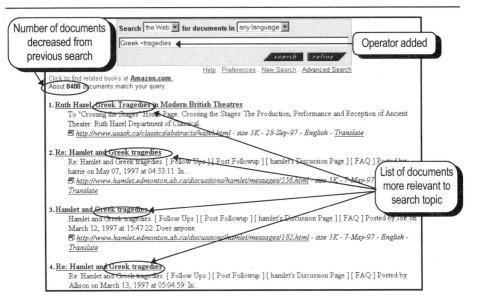

Labels within the image:

Number of documents decreased from previous search

Operator added

List of documents more relevant to search topic

- The number of documents listed is dramatically reduced, and the documents displayed display information that is more closely related to the topic, Greek tragedies.

- You can also *exclude* words by using the minus sign (-) to further refine a search and eliminate unwanted documents in the results. For example, if you wanted to find articles about Greek tragedies but not ones that deal with Hamlet, enter a search string like this: *Greek +tragedies -Hamlet*. Note the different results that display:

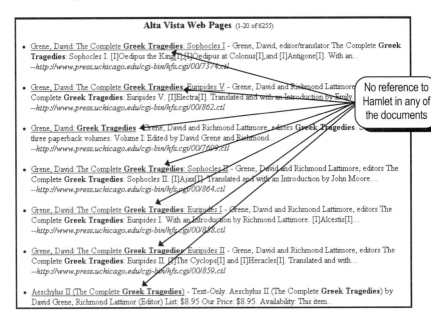

Get Help

- Check the Help features on the search tool that you are using to see what operators are available. Since there are no standards governing the use of operators, search sites can develop their own. Illustrated on the page 99 are samples of the help available for performing a simple search in AltaVista and Yahoo.

AltaVista Help for Simple Searches

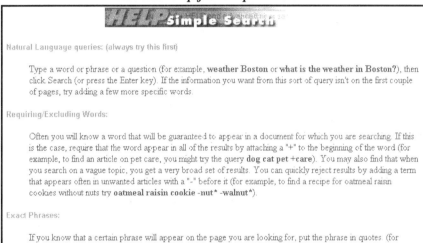

Natural Language queries: (always try this first)

Type a word or phrase or a question (for example, **weather Boston** or **what is the weather in Boston?**), then click Search (or press the Enter key). If the information you want from this sort of query isn't on the first couple of pages, try adding a few more specific words.

Requiring/Excluding Words:

Often you will know a word that will be guaranteed to appear in a document for which you are searching. If this is the case, require that the word appear in all of the results by attaching a "+" to the beginning of the word (for example, to find an article on pet care, you might try the query **dog cat pet +care**). You may also find that when you search on a vague topic, you get a very broad set of results. You can quickly reject results by adding a term that appears often in unwanted articles with a "-" before it (for example, to find a recipe for oatmeal raisin cookies without nuts try **oatmeal raisin cookie -nut* -walnut***).

Exact Phrases:

If you know that a certain phrase will appear on the page you are looking for, put the phrase in quotes. (for example, try entering song lyrics such as **"you ain't nothing but a hound dog"**)

Yahoo Help for Simple Searches

Tips for Better Searching

- **Use Double Quotes Around Words that are Part of a Phrase**

  example `"great barrier reef"`   [Search]

- **Specify Words that Must Appear in the Results**

  Attach a + in front words that *must* appear in result documents.

  example: `sting +police`   [Search]

- **Specify Words that Should Not Appear in the Results**

  Attach a − in front of words that *must not* appear in result documents.

  example: `python -monty`   [Search]

Search Engines: 21

Complex Searches

- When you first connect to a search site, the temptation to type in text and hit the search button is great. Resist it. Taking time to read and understand the search rules of the site will save the time you'll waste by creating a search that yields an overwhelming number of hits. Some of what you want may be buried somewhere in that enormous list, but working your way through the irrelevant sites can waste time, cause frustration, and be very discouraging.

- In "Search Engines: 20," you learned how simply using a plus or minus sign can create a search that gives a more pertinent list of sites. Now, you will see how to use operators to restrict and refine your searches even more.

Operators

- A **complex search** usually contains several words in the text string including **operators** that modify the text string. Operators are words or symbols that modify the search string instead of being part of it.

- Using operators and several descriptive words can narrow your search for information, which means the results will reduce the number of sites that display. This means the resulting list of sites should be more relevant to what you want, thereby saving you time and probably money.

- Each search site develops its own set of restrictions and options to create searches designed to locate specific information. What follows are some of the commonly used operators and how they are used.

100

Boolean Operators

- **Boolean operators** specify required words, excluded words, and complex combinations of words to be found during a search. Depending on the site, Boolean operators may be represented by words or symbols.

- The most common Boolean operators are:

AND The documents found in the search must contain *all words* joined by the AND operator. For example, a search for *Microsoft* AND *Internet* AND *Explorer* will find sites which contain all three words (*Microsoft*, *Internet*, and *Explorer*).

OR The documents found in the search must contain *at least one of the words* joined by the OR operator. The documents may contain both, but this is not required. For example, a search for *Web* OR *Internet* will find sites which contain either the word *Web* or the word *Internet*.

NOT The documents found in the search must not contain the word following the NOT operator. For example, a search for *Washington* NOT *DC* will find sites which contain the word *Washington* but none about *Washington DC*.

NEAR The documents found in the search must contain the words joined by the NEAR operator within a specified number of words, typically ten. For example, *RAM* NEAR memory will find sites with the word *RAM* and the word *memory* within ten words of each other.

- Suppose that you can't remember the name of the earthquake that occurred during the World Series in San Francisco in 1989. If you enter relevant words in the simple search function (using the plus sign) in AltaVista, here's what you get:

Click to find related books at **Amazon.com**
About **18368** documents match your query.

1. San Francisco Earthquakes
San Francisco Earthquake Links. The Ring of Fire/On Shakey Ground - An Earthquake overview. 1906 Earthquake - Before and After Films. 1906 Earthquake...
http://www.exploratorium.edu/earthquake/sf.earthquakes.html - size 2K - 11-Oct-95 - English

2. Why Earthquakes are Inevitable in the San Francisco Bay Area
Latest quake info. Hazards & Preparedness. More about earthquakes. Studying Earthquakes. Whats new. Home. Why Earthquakes are Inevitable in the San...
http://quake.wr.usgs.gov/hazprep/BayAreaInsert/inevitable.html - size 3K - 21-Mar-97 - English

3. Museums Reach Out With Web Catalogs of Collections /WW November 4 1996
Museums Reach Out With Web Catalogs of Collections. By Susan Moran. Earthquakes chase or keep many people away from California. The violent quake of 1989...
http://www.webweek.com/96Nov04/markcomm/arts_sake.html - size 9K - 17-Apr-97 - English

4. $A History of California Earthquakes (1 of 101)
Content Next. A History of California Earthquakes (Image 1 of 101) Earthquakes in the San Francisco Bay Region. Hayward, 1868. Vacaville, 1892. San...

Results do not answer the question.

- The results display several links to articles about earthquakes in the San Francisco area. If you click on one of these, you may find the earthquake you are looking for.

- Now examine the results of a more complex search using the same words, but using some of the advanced search options available in AltaVista. Entering the search string in the advanced search form of AltaVista displays the following:

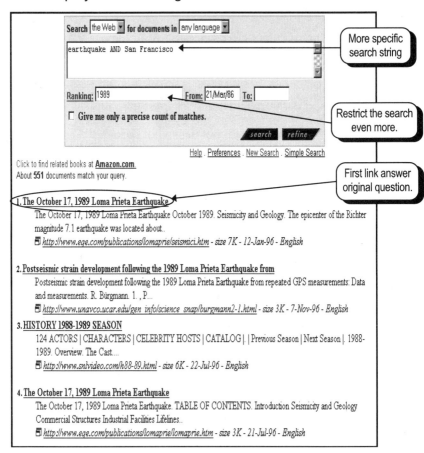

- Use the Advanced search function when you have a specific complex search string; otherwise, use the simple search function. AltaVista will automatically rank the order of the search results when you use the simple search function. When you use the advanced search function, you control the ranking of the results by entering additional search criteria in the Ranking box on the Advanced search form.

Plus (+)/Minus (-) System

- Boolean logic is the basis for the plus and minus system of constructing a search. If the plus/minus sign is not included in the search string, the search engine assumes that you are using OR. That's why when you searched for *Greek tragedies*, AltaVista looked for documents containing either *Greek* or *tragedies*.

Plus sign (+)   Placed immediately in front of a word (no space between the plus sign and the word) means that all documents found must contain that word. (This is similar to the Boolean AND function.) For example, note the results of a search for articles about earthquakes in California, using a search string like this: *earthquakes +California*.

Click to find related books at **Amazon.com**.
About **59247** documents match your query.

1. $A History of California Earthquakes (5 of 101)
   Content Previous Next. A History of California Earthquakes (Image 5 of 101) Earthquake damage in San Francisco Bay Region.
   http://www.johnmartin.com/eqshow/cah_0105.htm - size 399 bytes - 5-Dec-96 - English

2. $A History of California Earthquakes (2 of 101)
   Content Previous Next. A History of California Earthquakes (Image 2 of 101) State map with major fault systems.
   http://www.johnmartin.com/eqshow/cah_0102.htm - size 389 bytes - 5-Dec-96 - English

3. Earthquakes in California
   EARTHQUAKES IN CALIFORNIA. California is the highest earthquake risk area in the contiguous United States. Several large, well-known active faults run...
   http://www.eqe.com/publications/homeprep/eqkesca.htm - size 4K - 26-Nov-95 - English

4. $A History of California Earthquakes (16 of 101)
   Content Previous Next. A History of California Earthquakes (Image 16 of 101) Earthquake damage during the 1957 Daly City earthquake.
   http://www.johnmartin.com/eqshow/cah_0116.htm - size 411 bytes - 5-Dec-96 - English

5. $A History of California Earthquakes (9 of 101)
   Content Previous Next. A History of California Earthquakes (Image 9 of 101) Earthquake damage during the 1868 Hayward earthquake.
   http://www.johnmartin.com/eqshow/cah_0109.htm - size 407 bytes - 5-Dec-96 - English

Minus sign (-)	Place immediately in front of a word (again, no space) means that all documents found will NOT contain that word. (This is the Boolean NOT function.) For example, note the results of search for articles about earthquakes that do *not include* California using a search string like this: *earthquakes -California*.

Click to find related books at **Amazon.com**.
12985 documents match your query.

1. **IGS FAQs - Earthquakes**
   Q: I was born and raised in South Bend, Indiana and I remember experiencing a tremor on a Fall Saturday, right about mid-day, sometime between 1968 and...
   http://www.indiana.edu/~igs/faqs/faqquake.html - size 3K - 15-Jul-97 - English

2. **Index of /ftp/ca.earthquakes/1994/**
   Index of /ftp/ca.earthquakes/1994/ Name Last modified Size Description. Parent Directory 30-Jan-97 10:35 - 940106.gif 16-Nov-94 14:18 11K. 940106.ps.Z...
   http://scec.gps.caltech.edu/ftp/ca.earthquakes/1994/ - size 21K - 15-Aug-97 - English

3. **Index of /ftp/ca.earthquakes/1993/**
   Index of /ftp/ca.earthquakes/1993/ Name Last modified Size Description. Parent Directory 30-Jan-97 10:35 - 930107.ps.Z 08-Aug-94 10:17 40K. 930107.txt.Z...
   http://scec.gps.caltech.edu/ftp/ca.earthquakes/1993/ - size 18K - 15-Aug-97 - English

4. **USENET FAQs - sci.geo.earthquakes**
   USENET FAQs. sci.geo.earthquakes. FAQs in this newsgroup. Satellite Imagery FAQ - Pointer.
   http://www.cis.ohio-state.edu/hypertext/faq/usenet-faqs/bygroup/sci/geo/earthquakes/top.html - size 328 bytes - 15-Aug-97 - English

5. **GEOL 240lxg: Earthquakes**
   GEOL 240lxg: Earthquakes. Department: Earth Sciences. Instructor: Sammis, Charles & Teng, Ta-Liang. Semester offered: Fall Spring. Category: Natural...
   http://www.usc.edu/Library/Gede/GEOL240lxg.SammisCharles.html - size 2K - 22-Nov-95 - English

Grouping Operators

- The grouping **operators** join words and phrases together to be treated as a single unit or determine the order in which Boolean operators are applied.

- The most common grouping operators are:

Double quotes	The documents found in the search must contain the words inside double quotes exactly as entered. For example, a search for "*World Wide Web*" will find sites whose descriptions contain the phrase *World Wide Web*, not the individual words separated by other words or the same words uncapitalized.
Parentheses	Words and operators can be grouped to refine searches using parentheses or to define the order in which Boolean operators are applied. For example, a search for (*Internet OR Web*) AND *browser* will find sites whose descriptions contain the words *Internet* and *browser* or *Web* and *browser*. (Note that this is *not* the same search as *Internet* OR *Web AND browser*, which finds sites whose descriptions contain either the word *Internet* or both of the words *Web* and *browser*.)

Case Sensitive

- If you enter a word using all lowercase (hamlet), some search engines will look for both upper and lower case versions of the word. If you use uppercase in the search (Hamlet), the search engine will locate documents that only use the uppercase version.

Special Characters and Punctuation

- Special characters and punctuation can also be used to filter results in complex searches. The most widely used character, the asterisk (*) is used when a word in a search can have a number of different forms. Using the asterisk (*) as a wildcard tells the search engine to find documents that contain any form of the word. For example, if you create a search for blue*, note the wide range of documents that show up in the search results.

> Click to find related books at **Amazon.com**.
> About **800775** documents match your query.
>
> 1. Yahoo! - U.S. blue chips slash losses, Nasdaq edges higher
>   Yahoo | Write Us | Search | Headlines | Info] [Business - Company - Industry - Finance - PR Newswire - Business Wire - Quotes] Thursday August 14 3:20..
>   http://biz.yahoo.com/finance/97/08/14/z0000_21.html - size 4K - 15-Aug-97 - English
>
> 2. SI: BLUE DESERT MINING, BDE-ASE
>   BLUE DESERT MINING, BDE-ASE. Carlson On-line Profile | Started By: Dale Schwartzenhauer Date: Mar 9 1997 12:52AM EST. Investors should check out BDE, one..
>   http://www.techstocks.com/~wsapi/investor/Subject-13562 - size 4K - 15-Aug-97 - English
>
> 3. UBL Artist: Daly Planet Blues Band
>   Daly Planet Blues Band. The Daly Planet home page The only resource for info on this jam band from Hilton Head Island, SC. Band info, pictures, contact...
>   http://www.ubl.com/artists/009821.html - size 6K - 7-Aug-97 - English
>
> 4. takuroku blues
>   http://www.sainet.or.jp/~akihisa/ - size 242 bytes - 16-Feb-97
>
> 5. From Deep Blue to deep space: Take a panoramic look at Mars' surface
>   Take a panoramic look at Mars' surface. To view the image* below, you'll need to install IBM's PanoramIX plug-in for the Netscape Navigator browser. The...
>   http://www.ibm.com/Stories/1997/07/space6.html - size 2K - 30-Jul-97 - English

- Wildcards are useful if you are looking for a word that could be singular or plural (look for dog*, instead of dog to broaden the search results).

- Other characters that can help limit, filter, and sort results include: %, $, !, | (called the piping symbol), ~ (called the tilde), < (less than), and > (greater than). Check the rules of the individual search engines to see how, or if, these characters can be used.

Major Search Engines and Operators

■ Below is a table of the major search tools and how they use some of the search operators. Be sure to check out the search tips and help sections of the sites that you use frequently to see the most current search options. Search tools are constantly updating and improving their sites in response to users' needs.

Search Tool	Boolean operators	+/−	Grouping Operators	Case Sensitivity
AltaVista	✓	✓	✓	✓
AOL NetFind	✓	✓		
Excite	✓	✓	✓	
HotBot	✓	✓	✓	✓
Infoseek		✓	✓	✓
Lycos		✓	✓	
SavvySearch		✓	✓	
Yahoo	✓	✓	✓	✓

WEB RESOURCES

Use General Sites

◆ America Online ◆ Microsoft Network ◆ Pathfinder

General sites such as America Online and Microsoft Network have become much more than gateways to the World Wide Web. The best of these sites offer rich online content that can eliminate the need to surf and search the sometimes confusing and tangled Web.

At these general sites you can find the day's news, weather, sports, opinion, special interest features, and in some cases travel services, entertainment reviews, and other specialty information. Some sites also offer you the option of tailoring the home page to suit your personal needs.

These sites are bound to improve as they compete for additional subscribers with more and better content. Take advantage of these sites to get a great start to your Web experience every time you log online.

America Online

http://www.aol.com

 The home page for the leading commercial online service provides a well-organized directory of links to dozens of top Web sites along with brief reviews of each site.

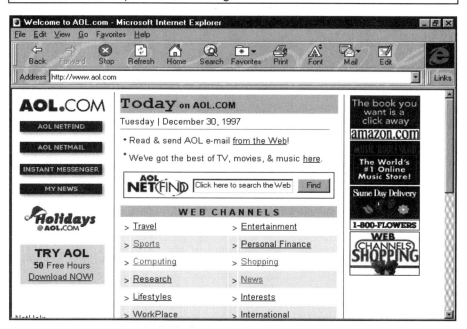

- The AOL Web site isn't just for Internet newcomers and home Web surfers. This site provides a good jumping-off point for any practical Web search.

- The AOL site has a comprehensive and well-organized Web directory, with access to dozens of links to many of the best resources available on the Web. Just click one of the AOL channels to see links to Web sites that AOL has selected as favorites along with a brief descriptive paragraph about each site.

- Though most of the channels are primarily oriented to a consumer audience, you can click the WorkPlace channel to see a very complete directory of business Web site links and associated site reviews.

- A few of the selected favorites on each channel are links to an AOL service available only to AOL members, but you will find many more links to sites available to you on the Web.

- A selection of AOL Web site reviews is arranged at the left side of each channel page. Click one of the review topics to dig down deeper and find more Web site links.

- Another nice feature at the AOL site is the easy access to search engine text boxes, where you can quickly enter a keyword search topic and click to find what you need. Each AOL channel typically showcases two or three Web sites near the top of the channel page by including search engine text boxes for those sites.

- Click the NetFind link to use the very helpful Time Savers directory. Here you will find links to Web resources for many common tasks such as Find an Airline or Hotel, Plan a Night Out, Plan a Night In, Manage Your Investments, Your Health, and Your Government.

- Links to AOL services such as NetMail (Web access e-mail) and Instant Messenger are also featured at the AOL site, but you must be an AOL member to use these services.

Microsoft Network

http://www.msn.com

 This leading computer software developer provides a broad range of online content for technology information, social issues, and entertainment.

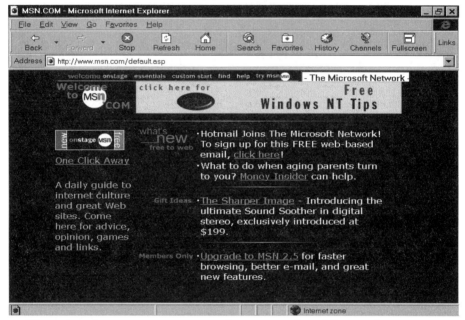

- There has been a pattern over the years when Microsoft enters a promising new market: Microsoft may not offer the first or best product, but after a while, the Microsoft product catches on and then overtakes the competition.

- The same pattern holds true in the commercial online service market. Microsoft Network (MSN) was supposed to take over the world when it was offered as an icon on the Windows 95 desktop several years ago. However, as many people who clicked the icon on their desktop found, the initial content available on MSN usually wasn't worth a second look. In addition, the network connections were typically slow and unreliable.

- Over the past couple of years, MSN's content has vastly improved, even if the network connections remain slow at times. MSN's wide range of consumer and information Web site offerings makes it well worth a stop on your online search.

- Topping the list of MSN sites is the award winning Expedia travel service. Expedia is an example of how much interactivity and rich

110

content can be delivered on a commercial Web site. Expedia's outstanding travel-booking wizard makes it a fine business and sales resource. Sidewalk is a wonderfully complete guide to nine U.S. cities as well as Sydney, Australia.

- Check out Microsoft Investor and Money Insider for a couple of the best investment and market sites available on the Web. Also, try the Computing Central site for computer forums, tips, software downloads, and industry news.

- The Mining Company is a new search site offered by MSN that offers the services of online guides to help you find what you want. Other MSN sites are consumer-oriented, but provide very useful and well-presented resources to help you find out about cars (CarPoint), movies (Cinemania), games (Internet Gaming Zone), music (Music Central), and shopping (Plaza).

Pathfinder

http://pathfinder.com

Use this easy-to-access directory to find Time Warner media Web sites such as Time, Life, People, Fortune, CNNSI, and Travel & Leisure. Perhaps the most complete and wide-ranging collection of current information available on the Web.

- Time Warner's Pathfinder site brings together all the news, information, and entertainment content of dozens of Web, magazine, and video properties owned by the media conglomerate.

- This site is a great source for news, sports, politics, and entertainment coverage, offering links to Time, CNNSI, People, Entertainment Weekly, Variety Netwire, Life, and AllPolitics.

- The above list is just a sampling of the interesting and informative resources available at Pathfinder. You can also find financial sites such as Fortune, Hoover's Business Resources, Money Daily, Money Online, Portfolio Tracker, and Quick Quotes.

- Get travel news and fares at the Travel & Leisure, WebFlyer, PlanetSurfer, and Magellan Maps sites. Net Culture sites feature PC and Web news and information.

- If you want to shop, click on one of the many Marketplace sites, including BarnesandNoble.com, CDNow, Fortune Book Fair, Internet Shopping Network, and Time Life Photo Sight.

- Pathfinder also provides free e-mail service, a financial calculator, community chat sites, a cyberdating service, and an investment portfolio tracker. This wide-ranging collection of sites may be one of the most comprehensive information sources available on the Web.

Use Directories and Search Engines

◆ **Yahoo!** ◆ **Excite** ◆ **Dogpile** ◆ **Open Text** ◆ **Other Sites**

If you're using the Internet for research, your main objective for being online is most likely to find a particular piece of information—fast. Although it can be a lot of fun, you don't want to waste time surfing the Web.

When you want information on the Web but don't know where to look, the best place to start is a directory or search engine. These sites help organize the vast contents of the Internet and the World Wide Web so that you can focus your search efforts and zoom to the exact Web site (or other Internet service) you need.

Directories Organize the Web

- Though they go about it in different ways, directories and search engines have the same goal—locating information online. Directories provide a map of how information is organized on the World Wide Web. Typically, they break the Web down into a number of categories—usually numbering about a dozen or so.

- Categories might include broad search areas such as Arts and Humanities, Business, Computers and Internet, News and Media, Science, and Entertainment. Beyond the main categories, directories typically break Web contents down into finer and finer subcategories. For example, the Business category might be split into Companies, Investing, Classifieds, Taxes, and more. Searching these layers of subcategories until you find what you need is called "drilling down" in the directory.

Search Engines Comb the Web

- Search engines provide you with readily accessible database search software that searches Web contents or, in some cases, directories or indexes of Web contents. You enter one or more keywords into the search engine's text box, click a button on screen, and then let the software do the work.

- Typically, a search engine will return a listing of results that match your keyword(s) as closely as possible. Many search engines include confidence rankings that indicate how closely the software thinks each result matches your keyword(s). Results may be links to Web sites or links to directory categories or subcategories.

- Search Web sites can include directories, search engines, or both. They may also contain news updates and other content found only at the search site. Each of these sites finds information on the Web differently, and that can help you find what you need faster once you have learned the unique benefits of each site's approach.

Yahoo!

http://www.yahoo.com

Yahoo!, the original Web search site, provides a well-organized directory of Web contents, a powerful search engine, and an ever-growing list of new features that focus on special interests.

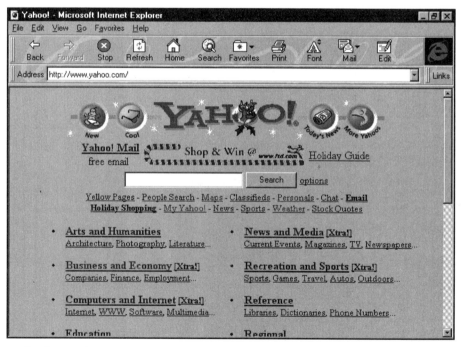

- Perhaps the most recognizable name in the Web searching business is Yahoo!, the granddaddy of them all. The site is continuously updated and new Yahoo! services are added regularly to expand the site. Click on the New icon at the top of the home page to see what features have been added recently.

■ What Yahoo! does best is organize the Web. The list of directory categories and subcategories on the Yahoo! home page has been copied by many other Web search and directory sites. If you have a fairly good idea of what you're looking for, click the category (or subcategory) link that comes closest to matching your interest.

■ After clicking a category link, you will see a page of subcategory links. Click one of these to drill down even further in the directory structure and narrow your search. After two or three clicks, you should start to zero in on links to specific Web sites.

■ You can also click on the Indices link after you have clicked a top-level category link to see a listing of Web sites that serve as link directories for that particular topic. For example, click Education, then click Indices to see links to sites such as Education Resource Links, Global Classroom, and ScholarStuff.

■ From the Yahoo! home page you can also click Today's News icon for a quick way to check the day's headlines. Click the More Yahoos icon to see a listing of other Yahoo! services such as My Yahoo! (where you can customize the site to your liking), Get Local (focusing on a Zip Code you specify), Yahoo! Chat (for online talk), and various Yahoo! Metros (focusing on major cities across the country). Click the home page Cool icon to see a directory of more off-the-wall Web site categories.

■ You can also search the Yahoo! directories by entering a keyword(s) in the search text boxes available on every page. You can search the entire Yahoo! directory or limit the search to the portion you're currently visiting. Remember, Yahoo! searches only its directories, which consist of Web page titles and descriptions, not the full Web. This yields more focused search results.

Excite

http://www.excite.com

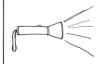 Excite features a tight directory structure and allows searching by concepts, which means you can enter conversational search phrases and get more targeted results.

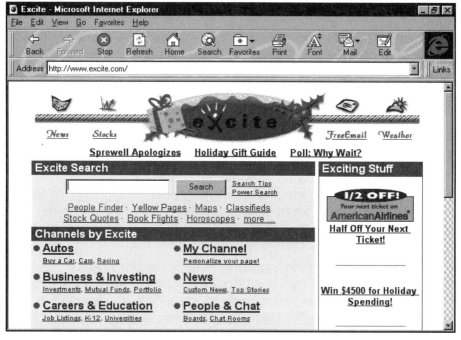

- After trying a few keyword searches, you may come to discover that Web search engines take your keywords very literally. The Excite Web site attempts to solve this problem by enabling you to search by concepts instead of by keywords.

- That is, the Excite search engine knows that words such as "coffee" and "cake" can have different meanings when they are used together from when they are used separately. The Excite engine also knows that words such as "play" can have many meanings, and it takes these into account when you enter a concept phrase.

- The bottom line is that you can use conversational phrases to describe what you want Excite to find. For example, if you're looking for plays by Arthur Miller, just type in "plays by Arthur Miller." If you're looking for sports plays of the day, just type in "sports plays of the day." Excite eliminates the process of deciding what the best keyword strategy will be to get the search results you want.

116

- Excite also provides a very tight Web directory that includes only three levels of categories. This is a reflection of the more narrow criteria Excite uses to screen sites indexed in its directory.

- You are guaranteed to find links to Web sites by the time you click three Excite category links. You can also read Excite summaries of each site that links to it. The net result for you is a quicker, more informed directory search than you can perform at other directory sites.

- Excite also includes links to features such as News (well-organized directory of wire service reports), Stocks (a business news summary page with stock quotes), TV (a table-style television guide), and Weather (national and local forecasts).

Dogpile

http://www.dogpile.com

 Use this search engine of search engines to look for what you want on 25 Internet search and directory sites.

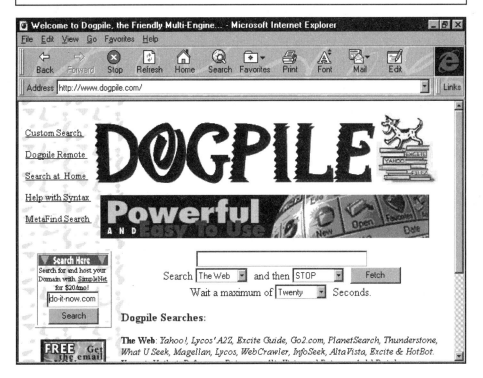

- Want to get the maximum coverage for your search? If you have trouble finding results at one search or directory site and have to jump to another, try Dogpile instead. Dogpile is the Internet search site that checks all the other important search and directory sites.

- You can enter a keyword search into the Dogpile home page and specify whether you want Dogpile to search the Web, FTP, Usenet, or newswires. You can choose to search a maximum of two of the above and then select a maximum time you want to wait for the search to be completed.

- Click the Fetch button and the powerful Dogpile search engine begins searching your selected Internet services three at a time. Dogpile searches 25 different services, including Yahoo!, Excite, Lycos, WebCrawler, InfoSeek, AltaVista, HotBot, DejaNews, and more. You can rest assured that you have thoroughly combed the Internet after finishing a Dogpile search.

- You can also specify the order in which you want Dogpile to search by clicking on the Custom Search link. Just select the service you want to search for each spot on the Dogpile search list from 1 to 25.

- Click on the Help with Syntax link to read a detailed how-to page for using keyword search operators such as AND, OR, NOT, and NEAR. Because some search engines support these keyword operators in different ways, you should check out the Help with Syntax page before constructing any complex Dogpile searches.

Open Text

http://index.opentext.net

Search every word of the World Wide Web with the Open Text engine.

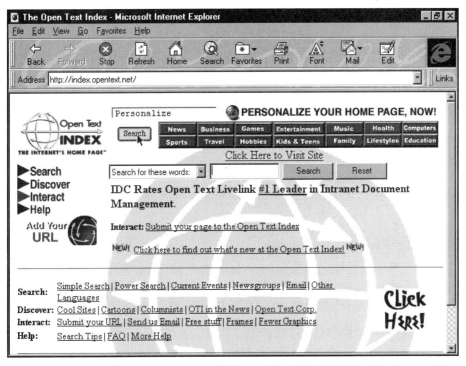

- When you really want to search the entire World Wide Web, use the Open Text search engine. Open Text treats the Web as one gigantic text file. Your keyword search in Open Text is virtually the same as using the Find feature in a word processing document, but in this case the document is the Web.

- From the Open Text index page, enter your keyword search in the text box. Click on the search button and wait for a results page to appear.

- Typically, you will get a large number of pages that match your search keyword(s). You can narrow the search by clicking the Power Search link. On the Power Search page you can enter multiple search keywords (one per text box), select where you want to search (narrow the search to titles, summaries, first headings, or

URLs), and link the keywords with search operators such as and, or, but not, near, or followed by.

- Drop-down list menus in Power Search provide choices for search locations and operators to make selection easier. Remember that the more keywords you use, the narrower your search will be (unless you connect the words with or, which includes all the keywords).

- You can also search current events, e-mail, newsgroups, and other languages. With a little practice and experimentation, Open Text searches can yield pleasantly surprising and highly effective search results.

Other Sites

Infoseek

http://www.infoseek.com

- Search any part of the Web quickly and easily with this widely respected search and directory page. It is easy to perform quick searches as well more complex searches at this site.

Lycos

http://www.lycos.com

- This full-featured search and directory site is famous for its top 5% reviews of Web sites. Its high-powered Custom Search page lets you hone in on the results you need.

DejaNews

http://www.dejanews.com

- This site searches Usenet newsgroups, the Internet's version of online chat bulletin boards. Handy for finding experts on a particular topic or just tapping into a discussion about a subject of interest.

The Mining Company

http://www.miningcompany.com

- This site takes a unique approach to finding information on the Web, with special interest sections led by "Guides" who specialize in a particular topic area. The Guide points you to links of interest, and you can also search the site by interest areas, subsections, or related sites.

One-Stop Resource Centers

◆ **Cool and Useful Student Resources** ◆ **Homework Heaven**
◆ **Schoolwork.org** ◆ **Other Sites**

Be thankful that there are dedicated people out there (many of whom are librarians or students) who are committed to making the Internet an organized and accessible resource for students. Many sites offer all the tools that you need to do research, write a paper, obtain information about what to do after graduation, and, as a bonus, almost all of these sites have links to pages that are just for fun.

Cool and Useful Student Resources

http://www.teleport.com/~burrell/

This site, created by a college student, is designed with high school students in mind. The links all take you to well-selected reference sources, not to a directory of sources.

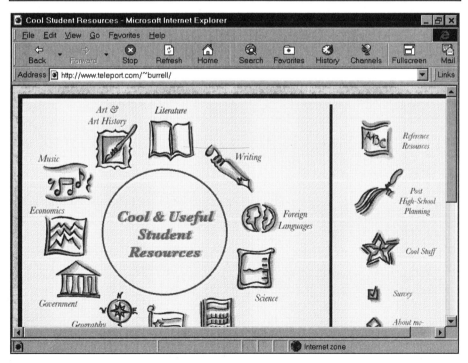

- Because a student created this site, the links are not only right on target, but the descriptions of each link are written in a student-friendly style and the cool links are really cool.

- The Writing resources are excellent. One of the links brings you to the Online Writing Lab (OWL) sponsored by Purdue University. Some of the helpful writing aids that the OWL offers include resources for writers, grammar documents, OWL info, and excellent Internet search tools (places to go when you want to start a research project).

- In addition to author-specific sites, clicking on the link to Literature directs you to book archives where you can download entire texts. So if you accidentally leave your copy of *Romeo and Juliet* at school, no need to run off to the library—simply download the play. Project Gutenburg, which is available on the Literature page, aims to get 10,000 texts online by the year 2001.

- Click on Reference Resources to open the door to several invaluable sources. For example, the link to Citing Online Sources is essential for anyone doing research on the Internet. Though the format for citing electronic references is not yet standardized, you must always cite your sources.

- Just for fun, click on Cool Stuff and check out the treasures: tons of animated images, comics, David Letterman's page, and more.

Homework Heaven
http://www.jumbo.com/pages/homework/

This site boasts over 150,000 "hand-picked" research links and 64 topic-specific search engines, such as the Biography Search Engine and the Dictionary Search Engine, to help you find just what you are looking for.

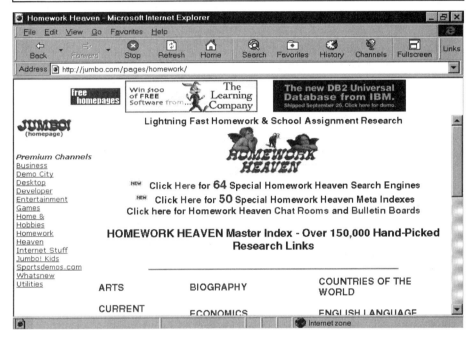

- It's all here at Homework Heaven. Sometimes you may have to click two or three times to get to the information that you want, but that's only because there is so much excellent material to sort through.

- Start by clicking on a topic that you wish to research. The first click brings you to a list of subtopics. From the subtopic list, click to narrow the results. By the third click you will land at either one *more* list of topics or the list of actual sources.

- Two of the most useful resources at this site are the extensive collection of topics under English Language and Reference Sources. Topics include basic grammar and punctuation rules on the English Language pages and the Reference Sources contain a selection of encyclopedias, dictionaries, and thesauri.

- Register to subscribe to Homework Helpers' "Top Five Research Sites" mailing list. Once you subscribe, each week you will be e-mailed five links along with site descriptions.

- At the bottom of the home page, you can access two enormous college databases: one contains all colleges and universities in the U.S. and the other is made up of colleges and universities abroad. Click on a location on a map to search any area for a school.

- From the colleges page, you can also click the Job Search link under the Business heading to access job databases, job sites, and related articles.

Scoolwork.org

http://www.schoolwork.org/

Created by librarians, this site, also known as Schoolwork.ugh, lists loads of great homework resources.

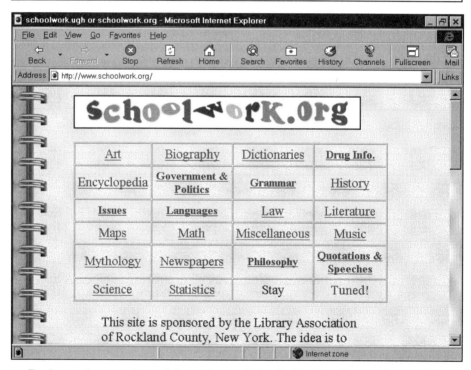

- Perhaps the most useful services of the Schoolwork.org site are the encyclopedia reference tools. These sources make obtaining information very student friendly. The Knowledge Adventure Encyclopedia works like a search engine; you type the subject in and then the encyclopedia searches a well-stocked selection of sources.

- Click on Science for links to some must-see sites, such as the Virtual Frog Dissection and the Nine Planets, which is a multimedia tour of the solar system. These sites are not only good for doing research, but they are also fun to check out.

- If you are interested in 20th Century literature, the literature page is the place to go. Click on author's names to access biographical information, photos, quotes, and bibliographies. The author selection includes many writers, such as F. Scott Fitzgerald and Gabriel Garcia Marquez, who are popular in high school and college literature classes.

- The Miscellaneous link takes you to several "miscellaneous but very handy reference sources" such as the home pages of the capitals of the states in the USA.

Other Sites

Britannica Internet Guide

http://www.ebig.com/

- Run by Encyclopedia Britannica, this site sorts, rates, and reviews more than 65,000 Web sites. Britannica offers access to the best sites on such subjects as art and literature, science and technology, history, and much more.

Study Web

http://www.studyweb.com/

- The resources on this site are designed for anyone doing any type of research. You can search their catalog of 37,000 well-selected sites, or you can click on a topic. The Grammar & Composition page is a must see.

Pitsco's Ask an Expert

http://www.askanexpert.com/askanexpert/index.shtml

- From this site you can e-mail or access the home pages of over 300 experts on various topics. So, if you are having a grammar emergency and need to contact a grammar expert or ask a teacher an online question, this is the place to go.

Kid's Place

http://www.nashv.lib.tn.us/kids.html

- Another great resource site brought to you by dedicated librarians. Kids' Place is about as organized as a Web site can get.

Writing Tools

◆ **Charles Darling's Guide to Grammar and Writing** ◆ **Elements of Style**
◆ **Other Sites**

Mastering the art of research is a critical part of writing, but being able to put all the information on paper, in a well-organized, well-written composition can be equally important. Even if you have a ton of information, you are bound to get poor grades if your papers are not well executed. Or, when applying for a job, if you cannot write a decent cover letter, you will never get that first interview.

Charles Darling's Guide to Grammar and Writing

http://webster.commnet.edu/hp/pages/darling/grammar.htm

 For everything that you ever wanted to know about sentence parts and word functions, this site provides it all. Written in very simple language and with links to lots of sample sentences, this site is a must see.

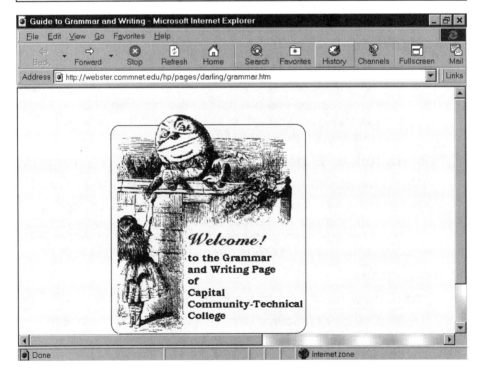

- Good writing is a fundamental skill that people often neglect. Even in the business world, a shocking number of people cannot write well-structured, grammatical letters. Work to become a strong writer. The first step is to memorize the basics, and the Charles Darlings's Guide is a good place to start. This site covers all the basics of grammar, including comma usage and clause definitions. This site is essential for anyone who ever has to do any writing.

- The problem with some writing guides is that they are difficult to understand. This guide is written in everyday language, making the definitions and examples easy to follow. With tons of examples, review points, links, and quizzes to test your skills, this site will prepare you for whatever you need to write. Also, links to other writing sites provide additional resources. Be sure to check out the link to the Guide to Writing Research Papers.

- Once you complete reading the information on a topic, be sure to take the related quiz to make sure that you are on target. The quiz commends you when you get an answer right and provides an explanation when you choose a wrong answer.

- Before you turn in any paper or send a cover letter to a potential employer, be sure to go through the Deadly Sins Checklist. The items on this checklist include all the writing sins you must never commit: sentence fragments, run-on sentences, subject/verb agreement problems, consistency problems, and faulty parallelism.

- Step right up, ladies and gentlemen, and for the price of admission to this site (which is actually free) view a rare and exotic 239-word grammatically correct sentence. Simply click on the link from the Run-on Sentences page and behold. You may get winded reading it, but it is something to see. And always remember: a sentence does not have to be long to be a run-on.

Elements of Style

http://www.columbia.edu/acis/bartleby/strunk/

 William Strunk, Jr.'s *Elements of Style* was originally printed in 1918. The aim of this text is plain and simple: to instruct on the rules of writing.

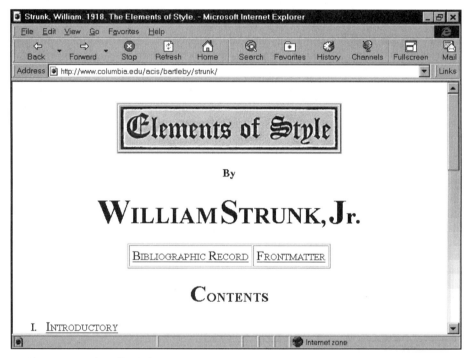

- If you need to find the best way to express your thoughts, refer to The Elements of Style's simple rules for writing clearly. Bookmark this Web page for ready access to the classic guide to effective communication.

- The opening page of the Elements of Style site is a table of contents. In addition to the Introduction, the topics are: Elementary Rules of Usage, Elementary Principals of Composition, A Few Matters of Form, Words and Expressions Commonly Misused, and Words Commonly Misspelled. This site covers the basic rules of the writing road, written in plain, easy-to-follow English.

- If you're wondering whether you should put a comma before a parenthesis or what a participial phrase at the beginning of a sentence should reference (or even what a participial phrase is), the Elements of Style is a source that you can rely on.

- Though the Elements of Style is a fantastic resource, it does not cover the conceptual aspects of writing a paper, such as organizing your information or revising a first draft of a project. See A Plus Research and Writing guide under the Internet Public Library for more information on everything else that goes into the writing process.

Other Sites

OneLook Dictionaries

http://www.onelook.com/

- For access to 1,369,501 words in 214 dictionaries, this is the place to go. This easy-to-use site encourages the use of Internet glossaries and dictionaries.

Webster's Dictionary and Thesaurus

http://www.m-w.com/dictionary

- Look up words or phrases online with this Web version of the classic American dictionary. Also includes a thesaurus and Word of the Day features, such as games, What's in a Name, Coined by Shakespeare, and Rappers to Flappers: American Youth Slang.

11 Rules of Writing

http://kbidesign.cnchost.com/fframe.shtml

- This is a brief but useful guide of the most commonly broken rules of writing.

Grammar Girl

http://www.geocities.com/Athens/Parthenon/1489

- Don't let the superhero on the home page of this site fool you. The Grammar Girl means business, and grammar is her game. Compiled by a technical editor, this site explains the rules of grammar and usage.

Study Web's Grammar & Composition Page

http://www.studyweb.com/grammar/toc.htm

- Study Web lists topics for all the basic composition skills, such as grammar, punctuation and spelling, and vocabulary building. However, because this site offers an abundance of resources, you may need to click on a bunch of links to find exactly what you need.

Libraries Online

◆ **New York Public Library** ◆ **Library of Congress** ◆ **Other Sites**

The Internet is changing the way we go about almost everything. One thing, however, holds true: if you want to find information on *any* topic, go to the library. Having the library online makes getting there even easier. And most library sites will lead you to excellent general links, resources, and interesting online exhibits.

New York Public Library

http://www.nypl.org/

 Whether you want to write a scholarly essay on the lifestyles of the rich and famous in ancient Babylon or just want to check out some excellent links to both academic and fun sites, visit the New York Public Library (online, that is).

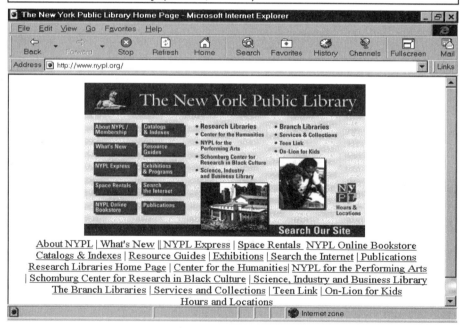

- The New York Public Library, which includes a collection of over 38 million items (11.87 million of which are books), is the largest research library in the United States. So, if you have research to do, this is definitely the place to go.

- CATNYP, the CATalog of the New York Public Library, can be searched by word, author, title, subject, periodical, or call number.

- The Teen Link link offers more everyday information and links addressing the basics: homework help, fun and games, career and college, TV and movies, and more. The librarians who have compiled and maintain these links do an excellent job of weeding out weak sites and adding new, good sites. Twice a month a cool site is selected and posted, and you can also check out past selections.

- From the Teen Link page click on NYPL's "Search the Internet Page." The New York Public Library maintains a huge catalog of Internet resources. From this catalog you can download electronic texts, research art and architecture, access links to selected current events and news sites from around the world, use telephone and e-mail directories, and much more.

Library of Congress

http://ftp.loc.gov/

 At this site you can search the holdings and major exhibitions of our nation's largest storehouse of information.

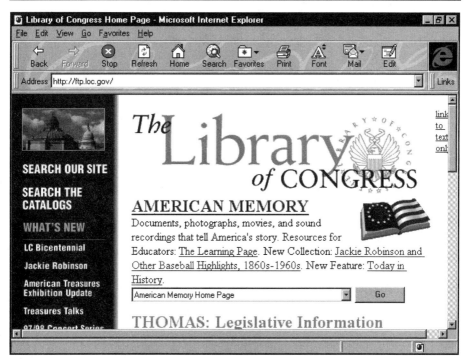

- You can search either the LOC Web site or the library's catalog of holdings. Though still under development, the Web site search contains an alphabetical index of the links within the LOC site.

- Click Search the Catalogs to begin browsing the LOC catalogs. You can use either a word search or a browse search. Some of the records found by the word search contain links to digitized materials available online. Browse search results yield only the LOC catalog information for materials.

- Perhaps the most interesting draw for this site is access to text and images from the library's ongoing exhibitions, the THOMAS database of information about the activities of the U.S. Congress, and the Learning Page for K-12 grade students.

- A nice new feature on the Library of Congress page is the link to Today in History. Click to read about events that occurred on the current date, years earlier. (You can also view the previous day in history and an archive of days.) For example, on December 21, 1997, the first day of winter, the Day in History was dedicated to the solstice and included motion picture clips from the late 1800s. The films were saved as .avi files that could be downloaded and viewed. The things that you will find on these pages—from Civil War photos to educational links—are always outstanding. If for no other reason than to check out Today in History, the Library of Congress pages are worth repeated visits.

Other Sites

- Most colleges and universities have card catalogs online and many major libraries maintain sites. Try doing a search for your local library.

Berkeley Public Library

http://www.ci.berkeley.ca.us/bpl/

- In addition to library reference material, this site links to an excellent search engine, the Librarians' Index to the Internet. You can also access teen links and sources that provide free e-mail.

Los Angeles Public Library

http://www.lapl.org/

- This site offers extensive research services. Other nice features of this site are a virtual photo gallery and a well-stocked list of links and resources.

Electric Library

http://www3.elibrary.com/

- For $9.95 a month or $59.95 a year, access a wealth of magazines, newspapers, journals, full-text documents, graphics, maps, and more. You can try out this online library service free for 30 days.

The Internet Public Library

◆ The Internet Public Library
◆ The Internet Public Library: Teen Division ◆ Other Sites

To say that the Internet Public Library is the best-organized, extensive, and interesting resource on the Internet would not be an understatement. The Internet Public Library is run by devoted librarians who see the Internet as an untamed sea of information. And they have made it their mission to put order to things. These librarians wish to serve the public by "finding, evaluating, selecting, organizing, describing, and creating quality information resources." And they have done an excellent job.

The Internet Public Library
http://www.ipl.org/

 From the Internet Public Library home page you can access links to an extensive selection of valuable resources—from the complete works of William Shakespeare to current publications and changing exhibits (neat Web pages) on topics as varied as Detroit jazz and dinosaurs.

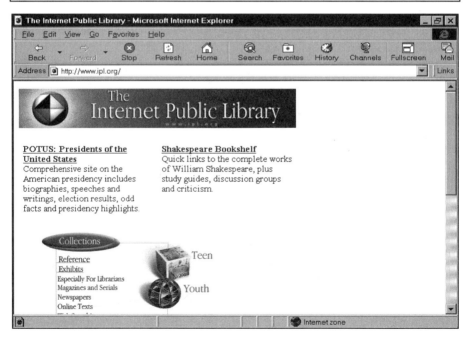

- The Internet Public Library is, in many ways, the superstores of Web sites. It's a good place to pick up information that you need, but once there, you will stumble on to other things that you didn't realize that you needed.

- If you need to do research, the Reference Center is a good place to start. When you access this link, an image map of the center appears. Here you can click on general Reference links where there are listings for dictionaries, almanacs, encyclopedias, and other reference tools.

- The Magazine and Serial link accesses IPL's collection of over 1,900 publications that can be browsed by either subject or title. The collection includes everything from scholarly journals to gossip magazines. The library's collection includes a great selection of publications on both popular culture and cyberculture.

- Click Online Texts to access a collection of 5,500 texts that can be searched by author, title, or Dewey Category. Many of the titles list complete texts.

- The Web Search link lists the Internet Public Library's favorite search engines. You can also access the Search Engine Watch, which lists search engine facts, a Webmaster's guide to search engines, search engine resources, and more.

The Internet Public Library: Teen Division

http://www.ipl.org/teen/

 The Teen Division of the Internet Public Library opens the library door a little wider—specifically to resources that are relevant to high school students.

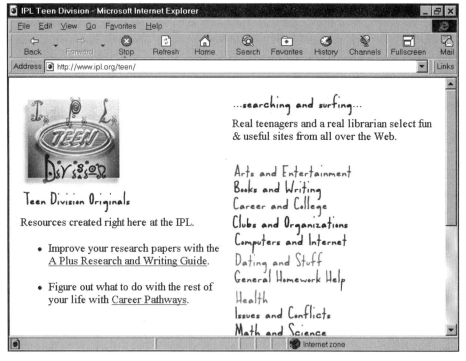

- The Teen Division of the Internet Public Library offers a nice mix of academic and social resources.

- For academic assistance, the link to A Plus Research and Writing Guide (http://www.ipl.org/teen/aplus/) is unbeatable. The site's offerings include a step-by-step guide to writing a research paper. This tutorial takes into account all aspects of writing a paper—from the stress that accompanies the writing process to forming a thesis or focus statement. The Research and Writing site also includes search skills and strategies, and links to online research, including OWLs (Online Writing Labs). And for the school topics that the A Plus Research and Writing Guide overlooks, the link to the General Homework Help page provides other great resources.

- When graduation time is approaching, the link to Career and College offers extensive information on getting financial aid, guides to careers, colleges and universities, and test preparation.

- In addition to the academic resources available on the Teen Division page, there are links to several pages that focus on social support. The subjects are both fun and serious, from dating and finding e-mail buddies to dealing with peer pressure and family problems.

- One thing to keep in mind when accessing some of the sites from the Clubs and Organizations link is that you never really know who is on the other end of an e-mail message or who you are *really* chatting with in the chat rooms. Be careful about giving your e-mail address out and never post your photo on a site. And most importantly: never, ever give out your real address, complete name, or phone number.

- The Teen Division of the Internet Public Library is an excellent place to spend time—if you have a project that you need to complete, if you need information on what to do after graduation, or if you have some extra time to spend surfing the Internet. Lots of cool links to excellent sites.

Other Sites

Career Paths

http://www.ipl.org/teen/pathways/

- This page is broken into three sections: Career Choices, Career Biographies (professional insight on different careers), and Career Preparation.

General Homework Help

http://www.ipl.org/cgi-bin/teen/teen.db.out.pl?id=gh0000

- Offers excellent homework resources.

Math and Science

http://www.ipl.org/cgi-bin/teen/teen.db.out.pl?id=ms0000

- Good general math and science resources.

So You Want to Go to College

◆ College Board ◆ Petersons.com ◆ Other Sites

Thanks to the Internet, applying to college has never been easier. Many one-stop college resource sites provide everything from financial aid information to school statistics to the actual application. With some sites you can fill out application information online and then send the information to several schools at once.

College Board

http://www.collegeboard.com

The College Board provides information on every subject related to the college-seeking process. Topics include taking the SATs, selecting a college, applying to college, and paying for college. The College Board's mission is to make college accessible to anyone who wants to go.

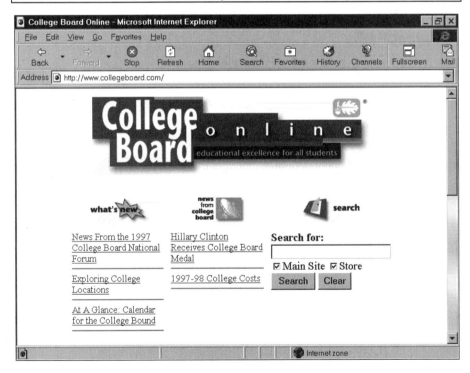

- This site comes complete with its own search feature. You can type in any college-related subjects, such as financial aid or dorm life, to find thousands of relevant articles. You can use the operators *and*, *not*, and *or* to refine the search. For example, if you type in *Financial Aid not Scholarships* your search will result in articles that only refer to Financial Aid.

- Click on online SAT® registration to register for the SATs. To register online you need to transmit credit card information. One of the new features of the College Board site is an online request form so that you can send your scores to admissions departments and scholarship programs.

- Click on college search to access a database of colleges that can be searched by location, name, or category.

- From the Students and Parents page, click on the link to college applications online. Here you can download a program for free with which you can apply to 351 colleges online.

- The Financial Aid calculator, found on the Students and Parents page, provides spreadsheets and surveys that help you figure out what financial sources you can rely on and where you fall short.

- On the home page, click on At a Glance: Calendar for the College Bound to keep up to date on what deadlines are approaching and what you need to do to keep on track and on schedule.

- When you need a break from all the forms, finances, and deadline pressure, click on the Student Art Gallery on the Students and Parents page to see some artwork created by students.

Petersons.com

http://www.petersons.com/

 Petersons.com's claim to fame is that you can obtain information about all colleges and grad schools at this one address. Use the Universal Application to apply to over 800 colleges online.

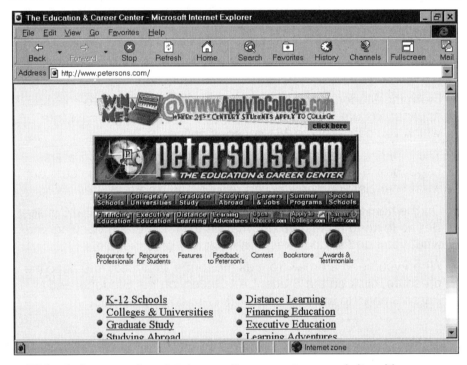

- This site's extensive database allows you to search by either alphabetical or geographical listing to find information on over 3,500 accredited colleges and universities.

- Click on ApplyToCollege.com to register with Polaris, an online management system for the college-bound student, and access the Universal Application. After providing basic information, you can begin. Features include private and secure online applications, an application manager that keeps track of the status of each of your applications, a student lounge where you can chat with other students, and a private messaging system so that you can communicate with admissions directors and guidance counselors.

- Using the Universal Application you can apply to over 800 participating schools. You only have to fill out most application information once. Be sure to look up each college that you are applying to in the database to check admission policies, deadlines, and applicable fees.
- Petersons.com also has an extensive online bookstore, most books published by Peterson's.

Other Sites

College and University Admissions Office Email Addresses

http://www.novakint.com/colleges/

- This site offers a comprehensive list of college and university e-mail addresses.

CollegeEdge

http://www.collegeedge.com/

- The site provides "everything you need to get into the right school for you." From getting started, to exploring majors and finance options, this site provides a wealth of information.

College Counsel

http://www.ccounsel.com/

- If you are exploring your educational options, this site offers lots of advice and resources. From this site you can request college applications to many colleges and universities.

Scholarstuff

http://www.scholarstuff.com/

- This site posts a college and university directory, information on standardized tests, chat sites, and much more.

Online Help with Entrance Exams

◆ Kaplan ◆ The Princeton Review
◆ The Educational Testing Service ◆ Other Sites

The dreaded standardized tests (SAT, PSAT, GRE) that are required to get into most colleges and universities have several support sites that offer more than just the facts of test preparation. These often-entertaining sites provide test takers with everything from tips on dealing with pretest stress to interactive flashcards.

Kaplan

http://www.kaplan.com

Kaplan is an educational company that specializes in test preparation, admissions, and career services. The Kaplan site offers a wide range of tools including the Kaplan Edge (Kaplan's free e-mail newsletter), a complete listing of all Kaplan courses (both online and live), information on financial aid, and more.

- Deciding that you want to go to college is often the easy part; the real work begins with the application process. Test taking, selecting a school, determining how you will pay for school, and getting it all together under extreme deadline pressure are the real challenges. The Kaplan site makes all aspects of the college admissions process more pleasant.

- The Kaplan home page includes links to specific pages for each standardized test. If you are about to take the SAT, for example, clicking on the SAT link is the place to start. Click on the practice link to access real SAT questions. You can then download diagnostic software (which is only free for a limited time) for feedback on your strengths and weaknesses.

- The 100 most common SAT words, excellent tips, and test taking strategies are some of the key subjects you can learn about at this site.

- The Kaplan Edge is a free electronic newsletter. Once you subscribe to the Edge, you'll get a math, logic, or English brainteaser and a vocabulary word via e-mail every day. In addition, every week you will be e-mailed a newsletter that includes reminders about up-coming deadlines, admissions advice, testing tips and strategies, and general info about how to keep cool throughout it all. If you are running Internet Explorer 4, you can add the Kaplan Edge to your active desktop.

- This site also offers vital information about financial aid. Start with Kaplan's "Tuition Impossible," a question and answer finance game. Then move on to more serious business. Click on Online Request Form for information and an application for an educational loan; click on Financial Aid Information for lots of basic information about the costs of college and available finance options; and be sure to click on KapLoan for Kaplan student loan information.

- When you need a stress-relieving break, click on the Links link, scroll down to the RATHSKELLER links, and have some fun. When you are ready to get back to work, be sure to explore the wealth of excellent links to valuable school-related resources on the Links page.

The Princeton Review

http://www.review.com

 In addition to the Find-O-Rama (provides college matchmaking), Remind-O-Rama (reminds you of upcoming deadlines), and Counselor-O-Matic (estimates your chances of admission at many colleges based on questions that you answer), the Princeton Review offers online practice tests complete with diagnostic review.

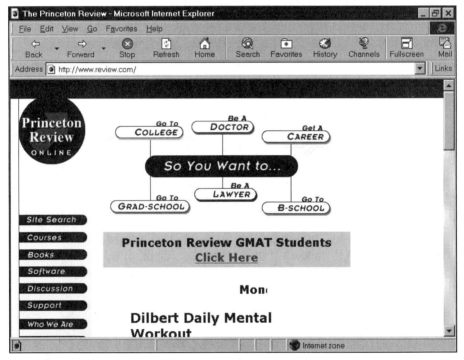

- The key to many of these testing sites is to make test takers feel at ease so that they don't really mind (or notice) that they are learning some great tips, tricks, and general information.

- In addition to the basic course listing and college admissions material, the Princeton Review page offers terrific material on the entire college process, including information on choosing a college and surviving college once you get in.

- On the college page, click the Tester link to access standardized tests online. Using Tester you can take complete tests, or just focus on areas that you need to develop. Once you complete a test, Tester provides a complete diagnostic review of your answers and your score.

- Though the Remind-O-Rama, "your virtual nag," may sound like a gimmick, it really is an invaluable tool. This feature can be accessed from the College page. Once you register and enter information about who you are and what you're planning to do, the Remind-O-Rama e-mails you to remind you of any upcoming deadlines or tasks that you need to accomplish.

The Educational Testing Service

http://www.ets.org

Just the facts (without all the bells and whistles) are found at the ETS site. For students who don't want to be distracted by nonessential links, this is the place to do testing research.

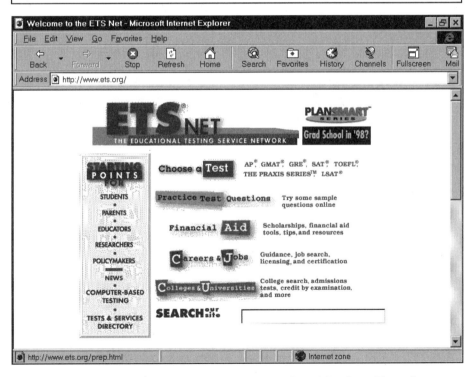

- Click on the link to Students to get started at this site. From here you can access many valuable links, such as online registration for the SATs and the College Board Online. You should definitely check out the College Board Online for test dates, registration information, testing tools, and other helpful information. Other informative links from the Students page include financial aid, fellowship, and internship resources.

- The E-zine can also be accessed from the Students page. This online magazine features articles, tips, and links to other interesting Web sites.

- Persistence at this site pays off. Sometimes several clicks are necessary to get to the information you need.

Other Sites

College Board

http://www.collegeboard.org/

- For one-stop information, this site provides dates, interesting articles, sample tests, and more. (See "So You Want to Go to College" for more information on this site.)

Test.com

http://www.test.com

- If you, a parent, or guardian is willing to send credit card information over the Internet, this fee-based testing service provides online practice tests for the SAT, LSAT, GMAT, and GRE.

College Essay Services

◆ The Mining Co. Guide to College Admissions - The Resume and The Essay
◆ CollegeGate ◆ Other Sites

Submitting an essay riddled with grammatical and stylistic errors to a college board can be the kiss of death. Fortunately, if you don't have an available teacher or English expert to review your college entry essay, there are many online services that, for a fee, will proofread and critique your paper. Other sites offer suggestions on how to create your own dynamic, well-written essay. The range of available services at these sites varies greatly. A note of caution: a college board may look down upon an essay that was obviously *not* written by a student.

The Mining Co. Guide to College Admissions -
The Resume and The Essay

http://collegeapps.miningco.com/msub14.htm

This user-friendly site posts articles and resources that deal with the college essay. Topics include sentence structure, grammar review, as well as insightful information on how to get started.

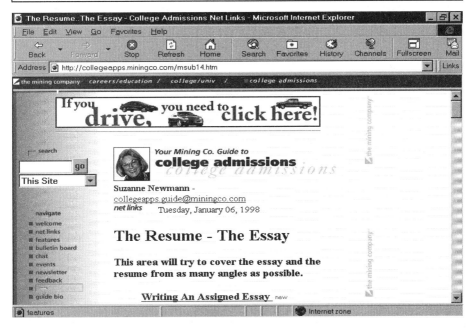

- Start by clicking on The Essay. This page lists ten basic and maybe even obvious things to keep in mind when you start writing any essay. Some of the eight commandments included in this section are "write them yourself and be yourself—be honest and forthright" and "the essay needs to be neat and complete, clear and correct, personal and positive."

- After going over the introductory pointers, click on Writing an Assigned Essay to review the parts of an expository essay (introduction, body, and conclusion) and read about forming a thesis sentence.

- Now, you are ready to start writing. But where to begin? Click on Writing Your College Application Essay for the meat and potatoes of constructing a solid essay. The information on this page deals with what to write and how to go about writing it.

- When you need a break from writing, click on The Perfect College Essay for a guaranteed smile. This is a humorous essay that has been in circulation for years. It begins, "I am a dynamic figure, often seen scaling walls, and crushing ice," and ends, "But I have not yet gone to college."

- The Mining Co. site lists excellent links on writing your personal statements, the letter of recommendation, ten tips for better writing, grammar and vocabulary links, style guides, dictionaries, thesauri, a free calendar tool, and much more. Check out this site for an abundance of excellent information.

CollegeGate

http://www.collegegate.com/

 Founded by a Harvard graduate with an impressive 3.85 GPA, this site provides fee-based editing and SAT services, well-selected links to college resources, and other college-related services.

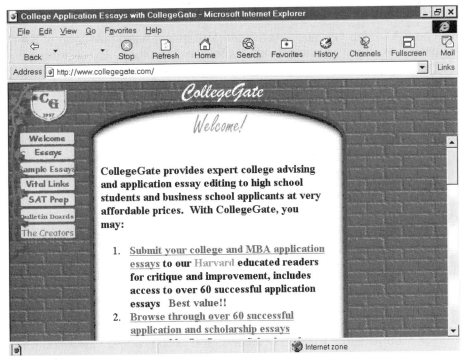

- Click on the Submit your college and MBA application essay to find out about editing services. The basic editing service provided by CollegeGate costs $49.95. For this sum, your essay will be reviewed by Harvard educated essayists. These said experts will spend several hours checking the essay for grammatical and stylistic errors. Included in the price is a suggested rewrite of the essay, a 2-3 page critique, and access to 60 online tried and true essays that can be examined for inspiration (and inspiration only, no copying allowed).

- If you are looking for motivation *only* without any editing services, click on the link Sample Essays. For $14.95 you will receive a variety of well-constructed essays. But CollegeGate warns "that copying the content of these essays constitutes application fraud and, if found, would nullify your application." Take this warning to heart—all college boards are aware of the services available on the Internet. Many may subscribe to essay services just to keep up to date on the essays that are in circulation.

- Click on Vital Links to access a great selection of college sources and services. Included in this list are links to financial aid and scholarship resources, a source to download the common college application, links to information on the top fifty schools, e-mail addresses for thousands of admissions offices, and much more.

- The SAT Prep link accesses CollegeGate's limited selection of SAT products, such as tutorial videotapes and services. By clicking on the Register/Pay for the SAT online you can link to the College Board site where you can register for the SATs online, check on test dates, and find some general pointers and tips on how to prepare for the test.

- From the SAT page you can also click on GoCollege, a sponsor of CollegeGate, to conduct a college search, find information on scholarships, take SAT and ACT online practice tests, and much more.

Other Sites

Essays and Research Papers
http://www.public.iastate.edu/~jgilchri/

- This free site offers basic guidelines on how to begin writing an essay. Topics start with understanding the assignment and coming up with an idea and then progress to forming a conclusion, making revisions, and proofreading. Learning how to write a good essay on your own pays off in the long run.

Cambridge Essay Service
http://world.std.com/~edit/index.html

- This site offers ground-up editorial services—such as fee-based assistance in forming a focus for your essay—as well as basic editorial and proofreading services.

IvyEssays
http://www.ivyessays.com/

- This service offers "inspiration by example." Translation: other people's essays as food for thought. Though selling essays is the main feature here, this site also offers fee-based editorial services.

Financing Your Education

◆ **Money Online College Guide 1998**
◆ **Education Services Foundation** ◆ **Other Sites**

Deciding that you want to go to college may be the easiest part of the entire college-entry process. The standardized tests, though not a lot of fun, can be conquered with a little bit of brain power, and filling out college applications just takes a lot of time (and a bit of money). For many people, funding their college experience is where the real work begins. Luckily there are innumerable sites that can help you figure out ways to pay. Looking at general college-financing sites is a good place to begin.

Money Online College Guide 1998

http://www.pathfinder.com/money/colleges98/

 This site gets right down to business: which colleges you can afford and which colleges will offer you the best education for your money.

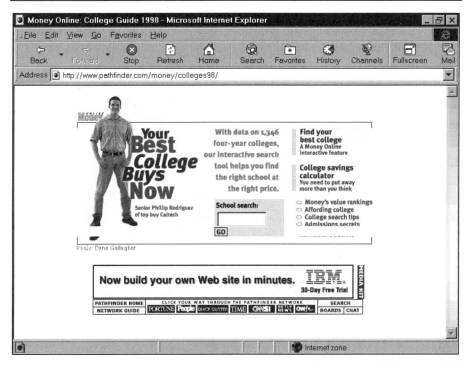

- Let's say you know which school is the school of your dreams. Try typing the name into the search text box. If the school is listed in the database, you are in for a lot of key financial information, including your dream school's tuition vs. the national average, financial aid statistics, basic information on average SAT scores, the school's contact information, and, if available, a link to the school's Web site.

- The Find your best college link gets you to a search engine that scans a database of nearly 1,400 schools. The search criteria are based on location, cost, financial aid, student body, admissions, and school services.

- Click on the Money's value rankings to find out which schools are excellent buys, dollar for dollar providing students the best education for their money. This site lists not only the top 100 all-around best schools for your dollar, but it also cites specific features like best women's schools and schools specializing in science and technology.

- The College savings calculator gives you the big financial picture—and chances are you won't like what you see. The calculator determines how much an education would cost depending on the type of school and the year of entry. For example, the calculator estimates that if you wish to attend a four-year private college beginning in 1998, it will cost you $85,349. (If that figure makes you weak in the knees, see the sites under "Financial Aid for College" and "Scholarships.")

- Two things to keep in mind while viewing this site: the text is often directed at parents, frequently making reference to "your child." Don't let this discourage you if you are doing research for yourself. The information that you can find on this page is too valuable. Also, this site only lists four-year colleges, but if you are interested in attending a two-year school you can still find lots of useful information.

Education Services Foundation

http://www.esfweb.com/

 The ESF is a non-profit organization that provides excellent resources on the costs of college and financing college. The site also provides information on general college preparation.

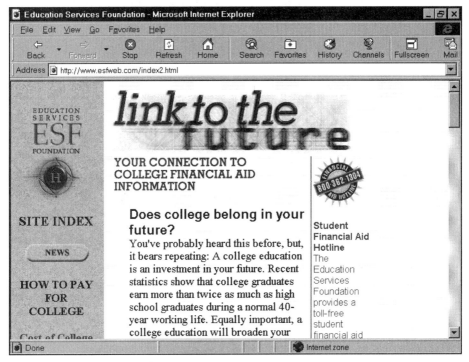

- Start by clicking on the College Calculator to access the College Cost/Savings Worksheet. This program takes into account tuition (depending on college type), the cost of books and supplies, and living expenses. The program then compares the total with the financial resources that you have available for your education.

- After you figure out how much money you will need to finance your dream education, explore all of the financing resources that ESF cites. This site includes information on scholarships, grants, federal loans, and work-study programs as well as other resources that you may not have considered, such as financing programs that the military offers.

- The EFS site is a good place to become familiar with the different components of financing your education, including terms and sources that you may not be familiar with. However, when you want to get to the heart of the matter—funding your education—other sites may be more resourceful.

Other Sites

- In addition to the sites listed below, check out the links and resources on the "So you Want to go to College," "Online Help with Entrance Exams," "Financial Aid for College," and "College Scholarship" topics.

The Index Map to Financing a College Education

http://www.householdbanksfs.com/indexmap.htm

- If you are looking for the how's, when's, and where's of the financial aid process, this site offers it all. This site offers a wealth of information, actual applications, and much more.

Personal Solutions

http://www1.usbank.com/personal/loans/student_loans/ student_index.html

- This site offers comprehensive information on financing your education, including lots of different financial resources and practical advice, such as structuring a monthly budget.

College Scholarships

◆ **FastWEB (Financial Aid Search Through the Web)**
◆ **Financial Aid Links** ◆ **Other Sites**

The nice thing about a college scholarship is that you don't have to pay the money back—one less thing to worry about when you graduate from college. However, in order to receive a scholarship, you usually have to be really good at something, like sports or math. Put your talents to the test; apply for a scholarship. The following sites focus on scholarships and fellowships, but you will also find other financial aid information.

FastWEB (Financial Aid Search Through the Web)
http://www.fastweb.com/

FastWEB boasts that it lists the most scholarships on the Web. The site also lists loans, work-study programs, and other financial assistance.

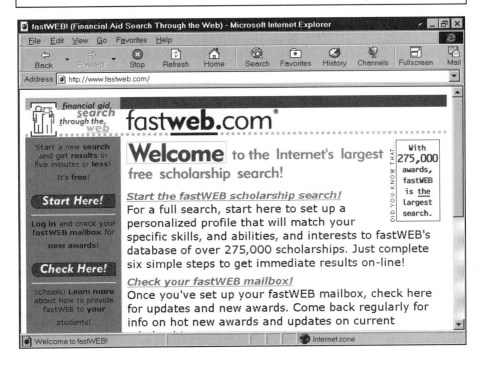

- To begin, click the Start the fastWEB scholarship search! You must first create a profile to use the search services. Simply respond to a series of questions and prompts to create your profile. Once you are set up, you can check your mailbox at any time to see if there are any new financial awards that meet your criteria. FastWEB automatically sends all new scholarships that match your profile to your mailbox. Featured resources and tips can also be retrieved from your mailbox. FastWEB claims to add 500 new scholarships to their site each day.

- Formatted forms or applications can be accessed directly from most of the scholarships. This means that you do not have to type a request letter from scratch. Just click on Suggested Form Letter to open a complete, addressed letter, with your name and address at the bottom. All you need to do is print the letter and sign your name. Other scholarships can be contacted online for application information.

- Click the More about local and federal aid link to find general financial aid information. Here you can view a list of resources and find out who is eligible for funding and where to write to get additional information or an application. This page also has frequently asked questions with responses.

- Click on Help and frequently asked questions for basic information on navigating the site.

Financial Aid Links

http://www.iwc.pair.com/scholarshipage/links.html

 Top scholarship sites can be located from this huge catalog of scholarships and sources. With a little work, this site's links can take you far.

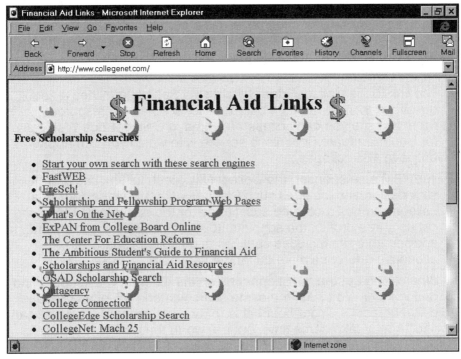

- Financial Aid Links is a great place to get started for free scholarship and college searches. The links on this site lead you to thousands of pages of information and advice on financial aid, student loans, fellowships, scholarships, grants, and other educational resources and organizations.

- Click on FreSch! to start using the power of this page. FreSch! is a free service that maintains a large database of available scholarships. The scholarship database can be browsed based on a search criterion that you provide.

- FreSch! also contains links to other scholarship searches, educational links, and "links to nifty sites that have nothing to do with education." In addition, FreSch! provides an excellent database of summer internships and some great application tips and tricks.

- The link to Scholarship and Fellowship Program Web Pages accesses a list of sources and links to school-specific funding, grants, and foundations. This site does not have search capabilities, so you need to scroll through the listings to find relevant resources.

- Click on ExPAN from College Board Online to access a database of scholarships, internships, and other financial aid services. The database can be searched based on a profile that you create. From this site you can also click on links to conduct a college search based on school name or degree, or a career search and questionnaire.

- The link to the CollegeEdge Scholarship Search launches a set of questions then searches a database for scholarship resources. From this site you can access Welcome to CollegeEdge Web Apps for Undergraduate Schools, a service with which you can apply online to 165 colleges.

- With IBM as a sponsor, the CollegeNet: Mach 25 link has a pretty slick design and includes such features as a 3-D virtual tour of a college campus (not to be substituted for the real thing). Once you set up a free profile, the scholarship search utilities are excellent. In addition, this site includes services to do college searches, academic reference material, and much more.

- When filling out the questionnaires on the different resources found on Financial Aid Links, the same search criteria will often produce different results. Your best bet is to try every resource that you can find. It may take some time, but it is worth the work.

Other Sites

Scholarships and Student Loans
http://www.dlc.fi/~frank/books/links/

- These pages list specific scholarships, sponsored by such giants as Coca-Cola and contain links to scholarship search sites.

The Scholarship Page
http://www.iwc.pair.com/scholarshipage/

- This site, which is connected with the Financial Aid Links site, contains a database of available scholarships that can be browsed by topic or searched by keyword.

Financial Aid for College

◆ **FASFA on the Web** ◆ **FinAID: The Financial Aid Information Page**
◆ **Other Sites**

Once you have sent in all your completed applications to your schools of choice, you should determine your need for financial aid by filling out and submitting the Free Application for Federal Student Aid (FASFA). In addition to the sites that deal exclusively with financial aid, most of the college-related sites have links that will direct you to financial aid resources.

FASFA on the Web

http://www.fafsa.ed.gov

From the FASFA site you can access and submit financial aid forms online, link to the U.S. Department of Education pages, and much more.

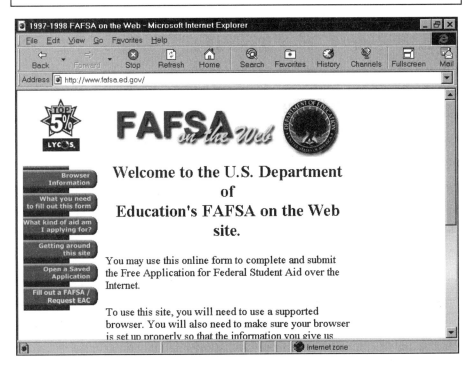

- Before you get started with this site, get ready to go on a scavenger hunt (you may need a parent or guardian's help with this). First find your social security card, then either your tax records or if you are a dependent, your parent's tax records. Click on What you need to fill out this form to see a list of the other items that you'll need to collect.

- Next, click on Getting around this site for the basic rules of the road for navigating this site. Be sure to read Browser Information about the browser settings. The online forms will not work if your browser is not configured properly.

- Now you can begin. Click on What kind of aid am I applying for to find out about the various Federal Student Financial Aid Programs. The link to the Student Guide provides a comprehensive listing of loan types and other general information.

- Click on Fill out FASFA/Request EAC to access the online forms and begin. Allow yourself at least one hour to complete the form.

- If you are uneasy about sending personal information over the Internet, then this site is obviously not for you. Everything from your social security number to your household's annual income needs to be entered.

- The Department of Education link accesses lists of resources for financial aid news, general information, products and services, and an alphabetical list of topics. You can also search this site and other relevant sites with the search feature.

FinAID: The Financial Aid Information Page
http://www.finaid.org/

Mark Kantrowitz's financial aid site provides not only detailed lists of financial aid programs, but it also includes extensive information on common financial aid myths, scams, and a glossary of financial aid terms.

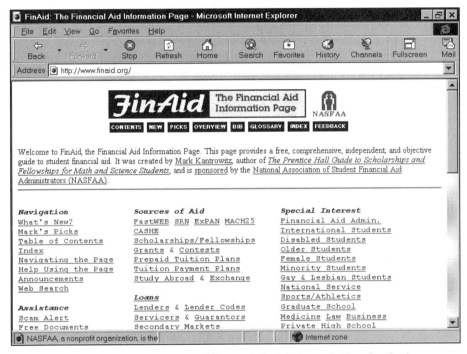

- This site is the superstore of financial aid sites, listing both the commonly known financial resources in addition to an abundance of obscure, yet valuable resources.

- The home page for this site can be a bit overwhelming, so a good place to start is with the Table of Contents link. The Table of Contents lists the same information as the home page but in an easy-to-navigate format.

- Regardless of what kind of financial aid information you are looking for, all of the information under Assistance is helpful. The Glossary of Financial Aid Terms is good to read through to catch on to financial aid lingo, and the Common Myths' links serve as an excellent reality check. If you have a specific question, you can submit it to Ask the Aid Advisor. A group of over 100 financial aid administrators volunteer time and resources to answer the questions.

- After looking at the Table of Contents, the best advice for navigating this site is to click on any links that interest you. This is probably the most comprehensive financial aid site available; it's just a matter of finding the information that pertains to you. Mark's Picks are always reliable.

Other Sites

- All of the school-related sites have links to financial aid sources (see "So You Want to go to College" and "Online Help with Entrance Exams"), but below are a few additional sites that provide excellent resources.

U.S. Department of Education

http://www.ed.gov/

- The Department of Education provides billions of dollars in loans, grants, and work-study programs. This site furnishes all the information and many of the applications that you need to get going.

Financial Aid Links

http://www.iwc.pair.com/scholarshipage/links.html

- This site posts links to valuable financial aid and scholarship resources. With this page the results are often hit or miss, but all the links are worth exploring.

Student Loans

◆ Nellie Mae ◆ EducationFirst ◆ Other Sites

For many students, a post-high school education would not be possible without a student loan. Getting a loan, though workable for most students, is a very complicated process. Your best bet is to check out lots of sites, both private loan services such as a bank as well as federal sites, and try to absorb as much information as possible. Then, if you are a dependent, talk to your parent or guardian about gathering financial information, or get your personal financial documents in gear and start the ball rolling.

Nellie Mae

http://www.nelliemae.org/

Nellie Mae, a nonprofit organization, supports the Federal Family Education Loan Program (FFELP). A giant in the student loan arena, Nellie Mae also provides private loans to students who may need funding beyond federal loan programs.

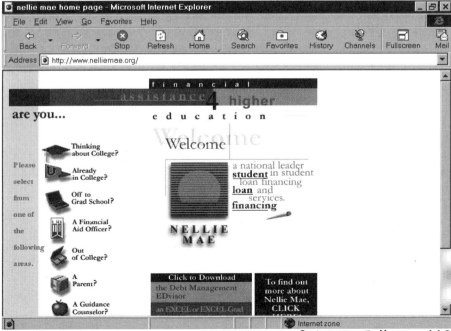

- If you are a high school student, start by clicking on Thinking about College? If you are feeling overwhelmed by the college application process, this is a must-see link. From Thinking about College you will find links to pages on how to plan for college, money-saving strategies, how to choose the right college, financial aid options, and more.

- From Thinking about College? click Pre-College Planning, to learn basic information that everyone needs to know, including FAQs, choosing a college, and answers to the question "Where do I begin." The Interactive Tools link features a college budget worksheet, a college budget calculator, and a monthly repayment calculator.

- The Loan Info link, however, is the most important resource, providing vital information on loan basics, loan options, and a glossary of all the new terms and acronyms with which you will need to become familiar.

- For additional resources, you can order free publications by clicking on the Order Form, and select Hot Links for a list of relevant sites.

- Once you have a better handle on the financial aid picture, you may wish to click on To find out more on Nellie Mae to see how Nellie Mae fits into your financial future.

- Now, down to business. Select an EXCEL or an EXCEL Grad Student Loan Application. From here you can download the actual application. The application also includes information on receiving a Federal Stafford Loan, which is money borrowed by a student, and a Federal PLUS Loan, which is money borrowed by a parent. Be sure not to rush through filling out the application; it is important that you supply correct information and that you understand the terms of your student loan. Remember, student loans don't magically disappear. They have to be repaid with interest.

- In addition to the actual applications, the Nellie Mae site posts timely articles on student loan and financing topics.

EducationFirst

http://www.chase.com/studentloan/index.html

EducationFirst, a joint venture between Chase Bank and Sallie Mae, provides services for both federal loans as well as private funding.

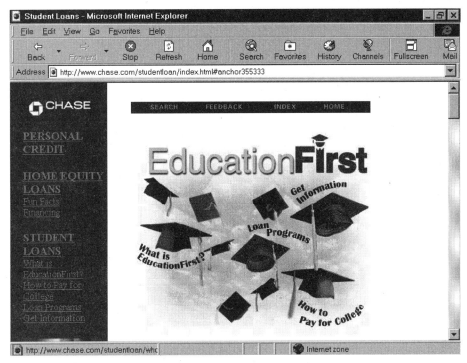

- One of the first things that you should do when you get to a loan site is try and find out about the organization providing the service. Click on What is EducationFirst to do so here.

- Then, click on How to Pay for College for basic definitions and listings of financing types, including the various classifications of loans as well as other resources such as work-study programs.

- The Loan Programs link gets you to the core of things—finding out what kind of loans EducationFirst can offer you. Click on the listed loans to get complete information. Find out about loan limits, interest rates, fees, repayment schedules, and other important information.

- Next, click on Get Information to open a request form where you can indicate which loans you would like to learn more about and which applications you wish to receive. Chase also lists an 800-phone number so that you can call with specific questions or concerns.
- Click the Search button to search the site by keyword or concept.

Other Sites

CSLF: Student Loan Foundation

http://cslf.com/

- This site is sponsored by a non-profit agency that finances and supports the Federal Family Education Loan Program (FFELP). CSLF aims to provide low-interest loans.

Citibank Student Loans

https://studentloan.citibank.com/slc/

- This site provides information on loan options. In addition, Citibank posts good general information about keeping on track and an extensive glossary on student loan terms.

ClassCredit Student Loans

http://www.classcredit.com/

- This loan service participates in the Federal Family Education Loan Program (FFELP) and provides various loan options for both students and parents.

Study Abroad

◆ American Institute of Foreign Study ◆ AYUSA
◆ Other Sites

Studying abroad can be an extremely worthwhile experience. In addition to academic knowledge, students will discover a new culture and history while gaining excellent life experience and independence. Programs are available for both high school and college students.

American Institute of Foreign Study

http://www.aifs.org/2index.htm

 Since 1964, over 800,000 college students and teachers have participated in AIFS worldwide programs.

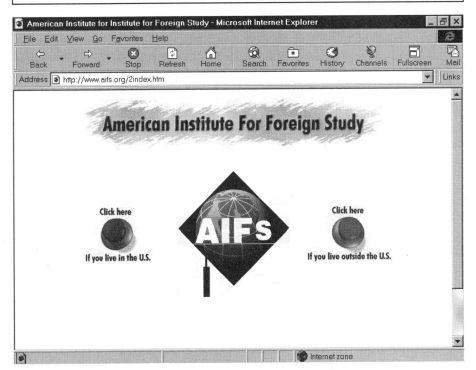

- The College Division of the AIFS offers programs for an academic year, a semester, or a summer abroad. AIFS strives to provide these programs at tuition fees that the average student can afford. In many programs, the only additional expenses are the transportation costs.

- AIFS sponsors programs at universities and colleges in Australia, Austria, the Czech Republic, England, France, Italy, Japan, Mexico, Russia, and Spain.

- From the AIFS home page, you must indicate whether you live in the U.S. or outside the U.S. For those living outside the U.S., AIFS offers various programs for students who wish to work or study in America.

- If you indicate that you live in the United States, you can then click on College Programs to select from various AIFS programs. Access the pop-up menu to see what AIFS programs are being offered. For each program, AIFS lists all necessary requirements—including grade point average and any language prerequisites.

- To get a jump-start on college, AIFS offers study abroad programs for high school students. On the College Programs page, select Pre-College Study Abroad from the Select a specific summer program here pop-up menu. Select from programs on architecture, art history, business, communications, drawing, economics, language/literature (English, French, Italian, and Spanish), government/political science, history, painting, photography, and theater/drama.

- The AIFS also has au pair programs. In return for childcare services, participants are provided a room in the home of a selected host family, meals, pocket money, airfare to Europe, and courses at a recognized university.

AYUSA

http://www.ayusa.org/

This study abroad program is for high school students between the ages of 15 and 18. AYUSA also arranges host families for international exchange students.

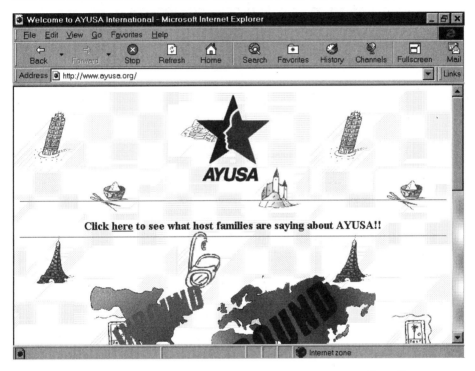

- AYUSA sponsors programs all over the globe—including Europe, the Far East, Eastern Europe, Africa, and South America. Programs span an academic year, a semester, or a summer.

- From the AYUSA home page, click the Outbound map to access the Study Abroad page. From the Study Abroad page click on Where can I go? to view an image map of the world. Click on a star on the map or on the country's name to find out about programs in that country.

- From the Study Abroad page check on the merit-based scholarships that AYUSA offers towards foreign study—some totaling up to $5,000.

Other Sites

Studyabroad.com

http://www.studyabroad.com/studyabroad.com.html

- This study abroad resource posts thousands of programs based in hundreds of countries. This site also provides additional information, such as a study abroad handbook, as well as links to other services and products.

The Online Study Abroad Directory

http://www.istc.umn.edu/osad/Default.html

- This study abroad service includes a searchable database of study abroad scholarships and "rock bottom" programs, which highlight low-cost programs.

Institute for the International Education of Students

http://www.iesias.org/

- This organization offers 22 academic programs in 18 cities throughout Europe, Asia, Australia and South America.

UR Study Abroad Internships in Europe

http://www.rochester.edu/College/study-abroad/europe.html

- This program offers internships supported with related coursework. The results are that the student gets both work and academic experience. Sponsors are available in London, Bonn, Brussels, Paris, and Madrid. Summer programs are available in London.

Resume Resources

◆ Kaplan's Career Center: Resume Styles
◆ JobSmart: Resumes & Cover Letters ◆ Other Sites

When you send a potential employer your resume and cover letter, most often that—and that alone—is what you will be judged on. A lot is riding on those few pages. Your resume is representing you, so don't just throw something together. A good resume is the only way that you can secure an interview. Give your resume a lot of thought, show it to friends or a parent for feedback, be sure to *always* spell check, and explore the resume resources that are available to you online.

Kaplan's Career Center: Resume Styles

http://www.kaplan.com/career/Resume.html

 Kaplan, a dependable name in educational services, also maintains sites that are career related. The information posted on the resume and cover letter pages helps you make a good first impression.

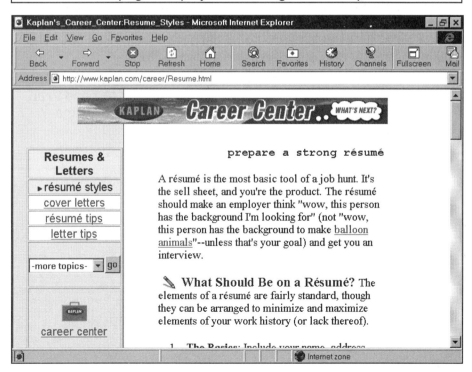

- When you build your resume, you don't want to tell the reader the story of your life. You just want to get an interview so that the employer can see how charming and brilliant you really are. The home page for the Kaplan's resume styles just lists the basics for both content and style.

- Start by reading through What Should be on a Resume? This section simply lists the 7 critical elements that you should include in any resume. A brief paragraph under each topic describes the ingredients that go into each section.

- Click on resume tips or Resume Tips-a-go-go for ten rules of the resume road, such as make your resume look good and avoid gimmicks.

- If your cover letter (which you must *always* include) is not well prepared there is a chance that the reviewer will not even get to your resume. Be sure to click on the cover letters link to see what a cover letter should and should not contain. At the bottom of this page, the link to Cover Letter Tips-a-go-go lists the ten dos and don'ts for preparing your cover letter.

- The Career Center link opens the door to the Kaplan Career Center home page. From this site, you can click to view a resume filled with mistakes to see if you can catch the errors. You can then see the resume, using the same basic information, done properly. This is an excellent exercise and should definitely be checked out. The same activity is also supplied using a cover letter.

- On the Career Center home page you can click on The Hot Seat: Wacky Job Interview Game. In this game you must respond to an interviewer's questions and try to get the job. If you select the wrong answer, you loose the game and the job.

- The Career Center also posts career tips, feature articles, and suggestions on how to deal with job-interview stress.

JobSmart: Resumes & Cover Letters

http://jobsmart.org/tools/resume/index.htm

> The JobSmart resume resources supports the idea that resumes are like shoes; one style is not right for everyone. Depending on your work or educational experience and what type of job you are looking for, there are different resume formats that may better suit your needs.

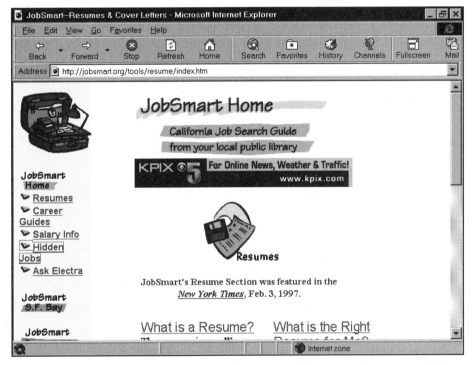

- After reading the basic information under What is a Resume, click on What is the Right Resume for Me? to get started. The four formats that are listed are chronological, functional (recommended for new graduates with not a lot of experience), curriculum vitae, and electronic (for posting your resume on online sites). You can view samples of both the chronological and functional resumes.

- Click on Selected Resume Resources on the Web to get to links to Yahoo!'s collection of resume resources (many of which are worth while), as well as links to general resources, first job resources, recent graduate resources, and others.

- The resume tips that are provided from Yana Parker are solid, however many of the strategies that she suggests are more relevant for people who have already had work experience.

- The Cover Letters link *must* be accessed. The material on this page stresses the importance of taking the extra time to prepare a complete and well-written letter. There is also information on what elements you need to create a good cover letter, things you should avoid, sample letters, and resources. Remember that you never get a second chance to make a first impression.

- Ask Electra (who is really a librarian with an ordinary name) is a service of JobSmart where you can e-mail job or career questions which are then posted and answered. Again, many of the questions that are featured were written by people who have had years and years of experience in the job market, but you will also find some questions written by high school students who are about to join the workforce.

Other Sites

Writing a Winning Resume and Cover Letter
http://www.gov.calgary.ab.ca/81/next/81yecpa1.htm

- This is a fun and informative site. Start by testing your resume IQ and then move on to what to include and what to omit when writing your resume. The 12 quick tips that are listed and the cartoon illustrations are right on target.

JobWeb: Resume Writing Tips
http://www.jobweb.org/catapult/guenov/restips.html

- This site provides resume basics and guides you through the steps of building a solid resume.

Resume Proofreading Checklist
http://www.careermosaic.com/cm/11online/11online7.html

- Print out this list and go through it before you send your resume out to prospective employers.

Rebecca Smith's eResumes and Resources
http://www.eresumes.com/

- This is an online guide that walks you through the steps of preparing an electronic resume. Includes information on creating electronic cover letters and posting the resume and letter once complete.

Job Sites Online

◆ **Monster Board Career Search** ◆ **CareerPath** ◆ **Other Sites**

When you want to look for a job you need not rely solely on the Sunday newspaper. The Internet contains hundreds of job sites featuring job listings as well as other career management information. Listed below and on the following pages are some of the Internet's best.

Monster Board Career Search

http://www.monster.com/

 With 50,000 job listings per day, Monster Board Career Search is the largest of the Internet's job sites.

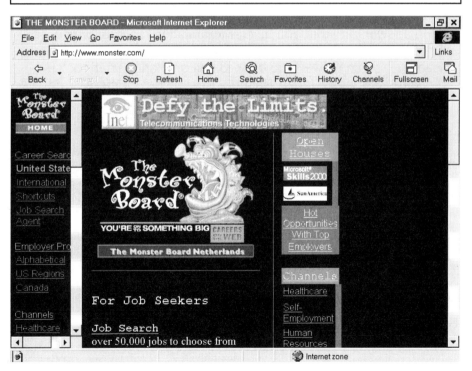

- Monster Board is the online job site of choice for people in their teens and twenties. The monster theme carries throughout, including the monster characters Thwacker , who "has compiled a monstrous list of U.S. career opportunities with more than 7,000 progressive employers," and Swoop , who "is a tireless monster that will zero in on perfect job matches, dive in and grab them, then deliver them" to you even when you are offline.

- Swoop, your personal job search agent, is a terrific resource. Once you have created a profile with Monster Board, Swoop will send job listings that match your profile to either your Profile In Box or to your e-mail address. You do not need to be online or reenter your criteria. Swoop does the work for you. And, best of all, the service is free.

- The database of jobs can be searched by discipline, location, or keywords and phrases. You can also search for either full-time or part-time employment. In addition, you can post your resume so that employers or recruiters can contact you.

- Use the Resume Builder to create an online resume. To create the resume you need to provide information, both fill in the blank and short answer, and then the builder formats the resume for you. Once you have created the resume you can apply to any of the job listings. You can always go back to edit or change your posted resume. (See sites under "Resume Resources" for more information on building a solid resume.)

CareerPath

http://careerpath.com

One of the most efficient and extensive job listing and career resources sites. You can search classified ad listings and leading industry employers. You can also post your resume so that employers can contact you.

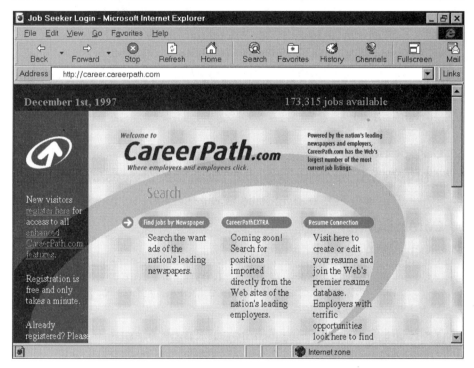

- The CareerPath Web site is simple and well organized and all the services are free. Take advantage of setting up an account with Careerpath so that you only need to enter your search criteria once.

- There are two databases for job seekers to search. The Find Jobs by Newspaper database is compiled from the classified ads of 30 different newspapers. The search criteria are based on keywords, job type, or location. On any given day the job bank contains nearly 200,000 job listings.

- The Employer Profiles database contains information about leading industry employers. Before you go on any job interviews, be sure to check this database to see if you can obtain information on the organization with which you plan to interview. Nothing impresses an interviewer more than an interviewee who has done her or his homework.

- The resume connection is a step-by-step service you can use to create an online resume. Once you have all your education and job experience handy, creating the resume is easy. When your resume is complete, it is added to the site's resume database. Personal information, such as your name and phone number, is not released to the potential employer until you read the job description and give CareerPath the OK to release any identifying information.
- Click on Career Resources for expert information on interview strategies, resume tips, networking pointers, and more.
- The streamlined interface of the CareerPath site makes navigating simple, efficient, and user-friendly.

Other Sites

Career Starters

http://www.asaenet.org/aboutasae/jobservices/cstarter.html

- This site lists entry positions with salaries up to $30,000.

CareerBuilder

http://careerbuilder.com

- A comprehensive job site with excellent career advice and such features as a free service that searches for job sites that match your criteria.

Yahoo!: Summer and Seasonal Employment

http://www.yahoo.com/Business_and_Economy/ Employment/Jobs/Seasonal_and_Summer_Employment/

- If you are looking for a summer job or internship, this database is the place to go.

News Sites

◆ The New York Times on the Web ◆ CNN Interactive ◆ Other Sites

Even if you don't have to do a report on current events, keeping up-to-date on the day's top stories is a must. In addition to fast-breaking stories, you can check out feature articles on fashion, movies, political cartoons, and more. There's no need to buy a paper or wait for a television newscast when you can get up-to-the-minute information online 24-hours a day.

The New York Times on the Web

http://www.nytimes.com/

"All the news That's Fit To Print" is posted by these news distribution giants. Updated every 10 minutes, the New York Times site brings you all the news, all the time.

- To begin using this mammoth site, you must first register. Registering is free and takes approximately 2 minutes to complete. Once you've registered, select a news section, such as Front Page or Sports, click on a headline to read an article, or click on News by Category to see headings that include international, national, metro, style, arts, and a photo gallery. From most articles you can access related articles and/or online forums. From Front Page you can click to read quick summaries of the day's top news stories.

- Click on CyberTimes to access all breaking technological news as well as past articles. This page also posts an excellent Internet glossary and guide and other news, views, and resources that deal with the electronic age.

- The New York Times site can be searched by today's articles or by all articles, which includes the CyberTimes.

- If you use Netscape Navigator as your browser, you can sign up for the free service New York Times Direct. This free service will daily deliver content from selected sections directly to your Netscape mailbox. Register for this feature by selecting Services from the home page, and then select the options under The New York Times Direct.

- If you are running Internet Explorer 4, you can include the New York Times as one of your channels. You can also have New York Times content broadcast directly to your desktop.

- For up-to-the-minute news, select AP Breaking News for the hottest stories. The features on this page are updated every 10 minutes.

- When you get tired of the news, select Diversions to test your knowledge on the Times' trivia quiz or view cartoons online. Also, if you are an at-home Times subscriber or are willing to pay $9.95, you can subscribe to the Premium Diversions service, which provides crossword puzzles, chess, and bridge columns.

CNN Interactive

http://www.cnn.com/

Get all the news you need from the worldwide leader in cable television news. You can also access more than 100 other sources, including CNN online services such as CNNsi, which is collaboration between CNN and Sports Illustrated.

- The CNN cable news network is widely recognized as the world leader in news reporting, so it makes sense that the CNN Interactive Web site should be as feature and content rich as the 24-hour news network's television coverage.

- The CNN Interactive site brings together the resources of CNN's own newsgathering team and the content of more than 100 other magazines and news outlets.

- The CNN Interactive home page presents the day's headlines with links to full stories. Also available from the very long home page is a menu bar where you can click on news topics of interest, including World, US, Local, Weather, Sports, Sci-Tech, Style, Travel, Showbiz, Health, and Earth.

- Links to other CNN online services from the home page include CNNfn for financial and business news, CNNSI for sports news, and allpolitics for political coverage.
- Scroll down the home page to view a complete directory of CNN Interactive site links, including direct links to stories under the main heading categories noted above.
- If the sheer volume of available news at this site is a little overwhelming, click on the Custom News link near the top of the home page. This link takes you to a page where you can register free of charge to customize the CNN Interactive page to suit your news needs.
- Select the Video Vault to download and view videos of current happenings. And, if you are feeling brainy, take CNN's news quiz to see if you are up on your current events.
- From the Video Vault pages click on the CNNPlus link to see a page devoted to personal features and news about topics such as Consumer, Community, Games, and Resources. Click on the Local link from the menu bar of any page to get local news updates from CNN network affiliate TV stations in your city.
- From the CNNPlus page you can subscribe to Special Delivery, the weekly e-mail update for CNN Interactive users. This service e-mails you special CNN Interactive sections, information on technological breakthroughs, resources, CNN programming highlights, and more.

Other Sites

MSNBC

http://www.msnbc.com

- Quickly scan daily news headlines and read the news you need in more detail. Also provides access to CNBC, MSNBC, and NBC television news.

International Herald Tribune

http://www.iht.com/IHT/home.html

- A true world newspaper, the International Herald Tribune's Web site is a great place to keep on top of world events.

NewsWorks

http://www.newsworks.com

- Get the day's news from more than 130 major U.S. newspaper Web sites.

Find Technology News

◆ CNET ◆ ZDNet ◆ AltaVista ◆ Other Sites

Learn the latest technology news by checking these sites. Each site includes in-depth feature articles on what the future holds in various segments of the computer industry as well as breaking stories about technological innovations.

There are many places to learn about computer and technology news on the Web. Nearly every general news and directory site includes a full slate of technology news updates each day. The sites covered here stand out, however, because technology is their primary focus.

CNET

http://www.cnet.com

 Keep up-to-date on technology information with this top site for computer news. Articles are entertaining and include numerous links to other tech sites.

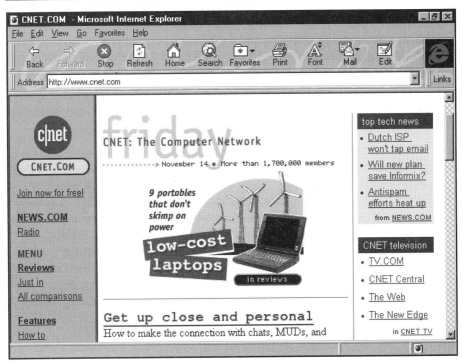

- CNET Central is a popular cable television show featuring news about cutting edge technology delivered in a friendly, entertaining format. The CNET Web site essentially follows suit. Here you can find great features about the latest innovations in information technology presented in a style that will appeal to the everyday user as well as the certified technogeek.

- The CNET home page includes links to articles on the day's top tech news as well as links to a multitude of very detailed product performance tests, reviews, and comparisons. Examples of recent product reviews include "Ten Bargain ISPs (Internet Service Providers) Compared," "Six Laser Printers for Under $400," and "Notebooks Under $2,500: CNET Reviews Nine Portable PCs You Can Afford."

- Click the CNET TV link to get information about the various CNET television shows, including the original CNET Central, The Web, The New Edge, and Tech Reports, which are brief tech news updates broadcast on local TV news programs.

- The Software Central page includes indexes of software ranked according to popularity (based on the number of copies downloaded from the CNET site), CNET editors' picks, and newest titles. This is a convenient place to see what's new and download it.

- The CNET SERVICES section includes several useful links such as Shareware.com, where you can find hundreds of shareware titles, and News.com, where a more complete listing of the day's tech news appears.

- The MARKETPLACE section includes links such as Buydirect.com, where you can purchase almost any type of software direct from the manufacturer, as well as a list of Specials, which are discount software deals culled from the Buydirect site.

- The Features section includes a wide range of "How To" articles, an entertaining set of articles called Digital Life, and a more expert-oriented set of articles called Techno. A recent check of the Digital Life section turned up entertaining columns titled "Ten technologies that will never work" and "Eight myths about the millenium bug." Among the ten technologies supposed to be going nowhere: Internet "Push" technology, ISDN lines, and the $500 Network PC. You may not agree with the predictions, but this is the kind of cutting edge tech talk that you will find regularly at the CNET site.

ZDNet

http://www.zdnet.com

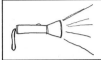

This is a very comprehensive and somewhat hip technology news site.

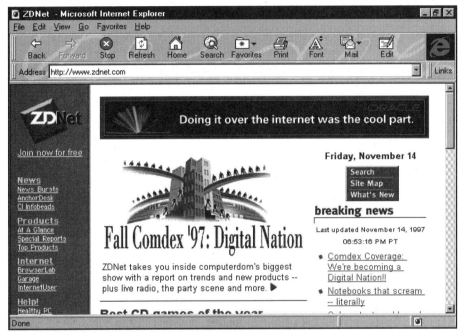

- The ZDNet site, run by Ziff-Davis, Inc., publishers of PC Magazine, PC Week, PC Computing, and Computer Shopper, among others, is a great place to search and access the content and resources of all these publications. With many of the most respected technology publications and columnists in the fold, this is perhaps the best site to find the latest computer news and opinions.

- The ZDNet home page features the latest computer news headlines. Click on News links to find News Bursts, AnchorDesk, and CI Infobeads. News Bursts includes the latest computer news headlines. AnchorDesk is a source for industry opinion with a bit of a chip on its shoulder.

- Almost every section of the ZDNet site includes a search feature to help you find information for the exact topic you want.

- The Products links provide you with one of the top computer hardware and software product review resources on the Web. Click on Reviews at a Glance to see a list of links to ZDNet reviews organized by product category. Special Reports provide a more detailed look at specific products, including beta previews and opinion pieces for products such as Windows 98. Product Awards is a clearinghouse for all of the many awards bestowed upon computer products by ZD publications editors.

- Internet links provide how-to Web user and developer resources, including The Garage, which features a selection of how-to articles for those interested in do-it-yourself Web page construction.

- Finally, the Help! Channel links may in fact be the best reason to visit ZDNet. The Help! Channel Healthy PC links include useful resources such as The Tip Zone, where you can enter a topic and search for tips and answers, Fix It Now!, Free Downloads for shareware, and an Ask the Experts section where you can consult with PC power users. Other gems include Online Video Demos and the Support Finder index of links to vender tech support sites.

AltaVista

http://www.altavista.com

 Good technology information site, but less comprehensive than others and colored somewhat by the fact that it is run by Digital Equipment Corporation, a computer hardware manufacturer.

- AltaVista was a fairly early entry into the Web search and news site category, and while there is still a lot of great in-depth tech industry reporting on this site, it's not as comprehensive as either the CNET or ZDNet sites.

- Also, the fact that the site is run by a major corporate player in the industry should give you reason to pause before assuming that you're getting a complete picture of what's new and where the tech industry is headed. A somewhat annoying ticker of Digital corporate news at the top of the home page is a prominent example of the bias in coverage.

- Still, there is enough here to merit a visit and search every now and then, especially if you're looking for information about a specific topic and haven't been able to find it elsewhere.

Other Sites

Wired

http://www.hotwired.com/frontdoor/

- Cutting-edge tech news delivered with a Generation X attitude.

Emmerce

http://www.computerworld.com/emmerce/index.html

- Part of the Computerworld news magazine site, this Web magazine focuses on the emerging field of electronic commerce.

Internet News.com

http://www.internetnews.com

- A down-to-business look at Internet trends and news.

Troubleshoot Computer Problems

◆ ZDNet Help Channel ◆ Indiana University Knowledge Base
◆ Internet Help Desk

What do you do when you receive the dreaded "not enough memory to perform operation" error message? How do you open a zip file? When you need answers to questions such as these, you can turn to the Web sites listed here. These sites provide detailed information that can help you troubleshoot computer hardware and software problems as well as find technical support at other Web sites.

ZDNet Help Channel

http://www.zdnet.com/zdhelp/hpc/

Get help from the combined resources and expertise of publications such as PC Computing and PC Magazine at this top technology site.

- ZDNet is the online home of Ziff-Davis, the publisher of popular computer publications such as PC Magazine, PC Week, and PC Computing. The site includes a great section called the Help! Channel that provides a front door to the combined resources and expertise of the Ziff-Davis magazines. Just click the URL noted on the previous page or go to the ZDNet home page and click on Help!.

- At the Help! Channel page you can click icons to Fix It Now!, Find a Tip!, or access Downloads! (the site tends to get carried away with the exclamation points, but it's a minor irritant).

- Clicking Fix It Now! takes you to a search engine page where you can type in your question or problem and then search the ZDNet database of tips and answers for the solution. The database is extensive, so you will likely find some help here.

- If you can't find the help you need, click on the SupportFinder icon to see an alphabetical directory of vendor Web site links. Search for the maker of the hardware or software you're having trouble with and click to get help. If all else fails, you can also click the ServiceFinder icon to find the closest repair shop to you.

- If you want to test the performance of your computer while you're at the ZDNet site, click on the SpeedRate icon. Click the Video Demos link to access video demos for basic PC maintenance.

- You will find a wealth of other resources at the Help! Channel, including Frequently Asked Questions, Ask the Experts, and online users forums. And don't forget to check out other parts of the ZDNet site for computer and technology news, information, and resources.

Indiana University Knowledge Base

http://kb.indiana.edu/

 Take advantage of this extensive database of computer troubleshooting and instruction provided by a Big Ten university.

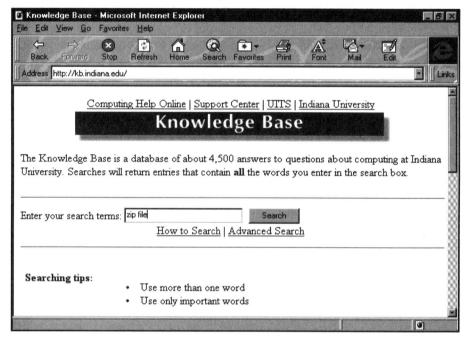

- Use the Indiana University Knowledge Base to answer questions you have about your computer. This Web site is maintained by a university campus computing center, and the breadth of information contained in its database includes more than 4,500 documents. This site is worth checking if you're having computer trouble or if you just want to learn more about a computing topic.

- Though you can search an index of common Knowledge Base topics by clicking on Menus, this list of links includes only a small portion of the available database.

- The best way to find an answer is to simply enter a topic or question. Avoid one-word and very specific searches for best results. Though some links and documents in the Knowledge Base pertain to the specifics of using computers on the Indiana University computing network, most files provide clear, concise general computing instructions or troubleshooting information.

- You can also click the Glossary link to see entries that provide definitions of computing terminology.

Internet Help Desk

http://w3.one.net/~alward/

Find troubleshooting tips, links to tools, Web guides, consulting services, and more at this free service site.

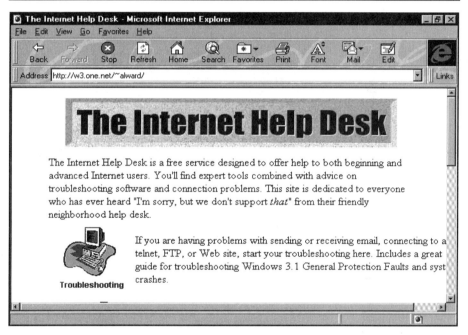

- The Internet Help Desk is a small site run by Amy L. Ward to, in her words, "meet my nerdish impulses," but it does provide some good links to Internet help.

- Click on the Troubleshooting icon to see charts that describe what to do when you receive e-mail, Netscape, Explorer, and FTP error messages.

- For example, imagine you have been receiving an "out of memory" error message when loading a Web page with Internet Explorer. Click the Explorer link and see that the cause may be that your machine's virtual memory may be disabled. The recommended remedy is to open your Control Panel and check the Virtual Memory system settings.

- The advice provided at this Web site is quick and easy to follow.

Buy Computer Hardware and Software

◆ **PC Magazine Online** ◆ **Internet Shopping Network** ◆ **Other Sites**

It stands to reason that the Internet is a great place to search for and purchase computer equipment. The number of technology-oriented Web sites makes finding bargains easy, and the advent of simple and secure online shopping sites means you can buy it better on the Net than at your local consumer electronics megastore.

PC Magazine Online

http://www.zdnet.com/pcmag/pcmag.htm

Start your search for great computer hardware and software deals with this very comprehensive technology site.

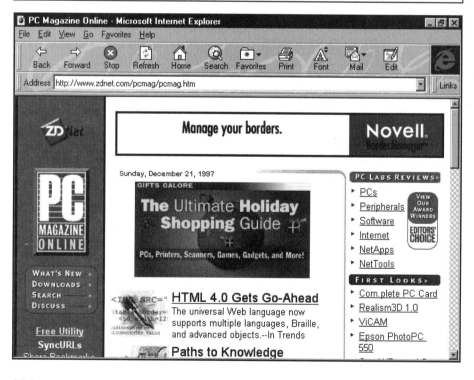

- There are dozens of sites on the Web where you can search for deals on computer hardware and software, but perhaps the most complete resource for your search is the PC Magazine Online Web site produced by Ziff-Davis as part of its ZDNet site.

- The PC Magazine site is a comprehensive resource for researching and making your next computer purchase. This site has the best selection of new product reviews, price comparison search engines, software downloads, and top feature columnists who can advise you about computer and technology trends.

- To make an educated purchasing decision, click the PC Labs Reviews icon or one of the specific hardware or software review category links underneath it. You can also click on the PC Magazine Editors' Choice Award Winners icon to read the editors' picks for best software and hardware.

- Click on the First Looks icon or one of the specific product links underneath it to read about the latest hardware and software to hit the market. Here you will find product reviews of the most cutting-edge computer products.

- The Trends link on the PC Magazine home page keeps you up to date on computer technology, with articles such as "Who's Winning the Browser Wars" and "What About Windows 98." The PC Tech link provides hands-on information for keeping your equipment on the cutting edge, and the Opinions link is where you will find columns from computer industry analysts such as John C. Dvorak.

- These are just a few of the tools available to help you in your initial product research, but there are a number of other, even more powerful tools to help you perform specific product feature and price comparisons.

- Click on the Products Channel for thousands of detailed product evaluations. The InternetUser provides development resources and how-to information for anyone who wants to use and build a Web site.

- The centerpiece of the buying experience at PC Magazine is NetBuyer. Click on the NetBuyer link to shop, compare, and buy hardware and software. Use the search engine to search by product category for the best deals. You can search either by product or by reviews. Click Specials to find hot deals or click on Basement for deals on overstocked or refurbished computers.

- After you find a price on equipment or software you want, it's always wise to check other sites to see if you can find a better deal. Even so, PC Magazine Online is certainly one of the best sites to use in making sure you get a great value.

Internet Shopping Network

http://www.internet.net

The same people who produce the cable television Home Shopping Network run this excellent Computer Superstore shopping site.

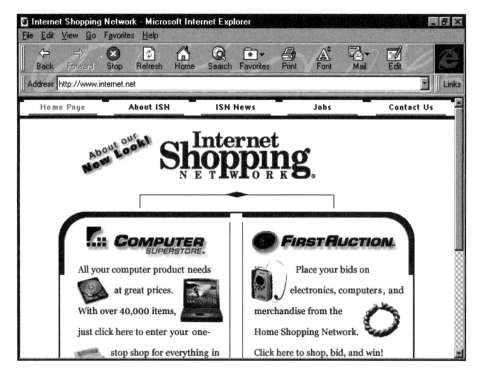

- Internet Shopping Network (ISN) is a great place to double-check prices against other shopping sites.

- Internet Shopping Network is a subsidiary of the cable television Home Shopping Network and was one of the first online shopping sites in the world. This pedigree of electronic shopping services helps make Internet Shopping Network an outstanding resource for getting the best deals available.

- Internet Shopping Network features two ways to buy: Computer Superstore and First Auction. Click Computer Superstore to view an electronic database of more than 40,000 items.

- Once you're in the Computer Superstore, type a product name into the Product Search text box to find information on what you seek to buy. Click on Hot Deals Central to see featured bargains.

- Making a purchase at this site is easy. View information about a product and, if you like it, click Add to Bag. The item will appear in your virtual shopping bag. Then click either Buy Now to proceed to a credit card information entry form or click Continue Shopping. You can also click Empty Bag if you change your mind.

- If you want to try a different way to buy, click on the First Auction side of the ISN home page. This part of the site features all types of items shown on the cable Home Shopping Network, not only computer products.

Other Sites

Software.net

http://www.software.net

- Software.net specializes in software you can buy and download all at one simple, secure site. More than 3,000 titles are available for immediate purchase and download, and more than 29,000 titles are included in the complete catalog for purchase. If you don't want to download a software purchase, you can have it shipped in the traditional shrink-wrapped box.

Insight Direct

http://www.insight.com

- Listed as one of Fortune's 25 "cool companies," Insight Direct offers great technical support, installation advice, and an easy-to-use interface for finding computer bargains. A search engine text box on the home page makes it easy to find a specific item quickly, and the Outrageous Deals feature e-mails you updates on limited time deals that often prove to be outstanding values.

PCWorld Online

http://www.pcworld.com

- PCWorld Online is another fine site for in-depth analysis of computer hardware and software products, similar to the PC Magazine Online site. Check here for an update on computer tech news, features, and columns from PC World magazine. Click the Top 400 Link for the top 400 software and hardware product reviews.

Issues and Conflict

◆ **Adolescence Directory On-Line** ◆ **Teen Health Web Site**
◆ **Other Sites**

One of the wonderful things about the Internet is that you can explore topics and issues—things that are really personal to you—without having the entire world knowing all about your private concerns. The Internet provides a wealth of valuable resources that deal with health issues and concerns, depression, family problems, eating disorders, and much more. Perhaps the best thing about exploring these resources is simply the reassurance that you are not alone.

Adolescence Directory On-Line

http://education.indiana.edu/cas/adol/adol.html

 This award-winning site's topics and links provide guidance and assistance for some of life's most difficult issues.

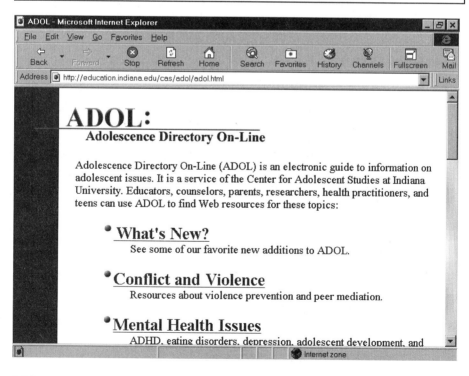

ADOL - Microsoft Internet Explorer

File Edit View Go Favorites Help

Back Forward Stop Refresh Home Search Favorites History Channels Fullscreen Mail

Address http://education.indiana.edu/cas/adol/adol.html Links

ADOL:
Adolescence Directory On-Line

Adolescence Directory On-Line (ADOL) is an electronic guide to information on adolescent issues. It is a service of the Center for Adolescent Studies at Indiana University. Educators, counselors, parents, researchers, health practitioners, and teens can use ADOL to find Web resources for these topics:

● **What's New?**
   See some of our favorite new additions to ADOL.

● **Conflict and Violence**
   Resources about violence prevention and peer mediation.

● **Mental Health Issues**
   ADHD, eating disorders, depression, adolescent development, and

Internet zone

- Of all the online resources that address the difficult issues associated with mental and physical well being, this site's listings are the most comprehensive.

- The best advice for navigating this site is to click on any topic that you would like to find out more about. From each main topic on the ADOL home page, you connect to a page listing numerous related subjects. From there, you may click on links that take you to related Web sites, or on a subject that opens a list of more links. ADOL provides descriptions of all linked Web sites to help you find the specific resources you may need.

- In addition to the mental and physical health services, there is a section geared exclusively to teens. E-zines, homework helpers, information on organizations and clubs, and some fun sites can be accessed from the Teens Only portion of the ADOL site.

Teen Health Web Site

http://chebucto.ns.ca/Health/TeenHealth/index.html

The Teen Health page surveyed teens to find out what health topics concern them most. The page aims to distribute health and medical information to the public.

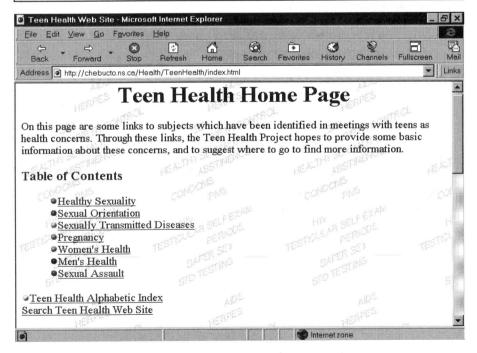

- The staff of the Dalhousie Medical School worked with local teens to find out what health and sexuality issues concerned them most. These topics provide the basis for the Teen Health Home Page.

- Each topic on the home page leads to a table of contents with the specifics of the topic. Many of the main links access another table of contents with additional resources. And many of the articles include hyperlinks to additional information or definitions.

- The topics on the Teen Health page mostly address sexual health and development issues; for more general concerns, go to the Adolescence Directory On-Line page (see pages 196-197).

Other Sites

Go Ask Alice

http://www.columbia.edu/cu/healthwise/alice.html

- This site is an interactive question and answer health service sponsored by Columbia University. People can submit questions on such topics as sexual health, relationships, emotional well being, drugs, and alcohol, and then Alice answers selected questions and posts the responses.

How 2b DifferEnT

http://www.schoolnet.ca/lang_soc/different/ diffmain.html#menu

- A teenager who felt different within her community created this site. Topics explore how to cope with these feelings of exclusion. Visitors are invited to share their own experiences.

Brochure Resource Library

http://www.nau.edu/~fronske/broch.html

- View brochures on various health topics—from self-esteem to common cold care.

Appendix A: Viruses

◆ **Introduction** ◆ **Origins of Viruses** ◆ **Categories of Viruses**
◆ **Timing of Viruses** ◆ **Virus Symptoms** ◆ **Precautions**

Introduction

- Viruses are malicious programs written to attempt some form of deliberate destruction to someone's computer. They are instructions or code that have been written to reproduce as they attach themselves to other programs without the user's knowledge. Viruses can be programmed to do anything a computer can do. Viruses are a nuisance, but if you know how they work and take the necessary precautions to deal with them, they are manageable. It is essential that you understand the nature of these programs, how they work, and how they can be disinfected. No one is exempt from viruses; strict precautions and anti-virus programs are the answer.

- Viruses are potentially destructive to one file or to an entire hard disk, whether the file or hard disk is one used in a standalone computer or in a multi-user network. Like biological viruses, computer viruses need a host, or a program, to infect. Once infection has been transferred, the viruses can spread like wildfire through the entire library of files. Like human sickness, viruses come in many different forms; some are more debilitating than others.

Origins of Viruses

- How do you get a virus? They can come from a couple of places:
  - An infected diskette
  - Downloading an infected file from a bulletin board, the Internet, or an online service
- Knowing where viruses are likely to be introduced will make you sensitive to the possibility of getting one.

Categories of Viruses

- Viruses come in two categories:
  - Boot Sector Viruses
  - File Viruses

- **Boot Sector Viruses** may also be called System Sector viruses because they attack the system sector. System or boot sectors contain programs that are executed when the PC is booted. System or boot sectors do not have files. The hardware reads information in the area in the bootup sections of the computer. Because these sectors are vital for PC operation, they are prime target areas for viruses.

- Two types of system sectors exist: DOS sectors and partition sectors. PCs characteristically have a DOS sector and one or more sectors created by the partitioning command, FDISK, or proprietary partitioning software. Partition sectors are commonly called Master Boot Records (MBR). Viruses that attach to these areas are seriously damaging ones.

- **File Viruses** are more commonly found. Characteristically, a file virus infects by overwriting part or all of a file.

Timing of Viruses

- Viruses come in many sizes and with various symptoms. For example, a virus may attach itself to a program immediately and begin to infect an entire hard disk. Or the virus can be written to attack at a specific time. For example, the Michelangelo virus strikes on his birthday each May.

- Some viruses are written so that they delay letting you know of their existence until they have done major damage.

Virus Symptoms

- How can you tell if you have a virus? Hopefully, you will install anti-virus software in your PC that will identify viruses and make you aware immediately upon entry to your system. Otherwise, you may experience different symptoms such as:
  - Slow processing
  - Animation or sound appearing out of nowhere
  - Unusually heavy disk activity
  - Odd changes in files
  - Unusual printer activity

Precautions

- Most viruses spread when you have booted the computer from an infected diskette. A healthy precaution here would be to boot only from the hard drive.

    - Backup all files. At least two complete backups are recommended.

    - Even new software can come with a virus; scan every diskette before use.

    - Mark all software program attributes as read only.

    - Research and update anti-virus products on an ongoing basis to have the latest protection.

    - Since there are many types of viruses, one type of anti-virus protection won't disinfect all viruses. The safest approach is to install a multiple anti-virus program library.

Appendix B: Emoticons and Abbreviations

Since you cannot see the people with whom you communicate on the Internet, here are some symbols you can use to convey emotion in your messages. This section also contains some acronyms that you will encounter in Internet messages (such as e-mail, newsgroup messages, and chat room discussions). Be sure to use these cute symbols and abbreviations *only* in your personal communications.

For more emoticons and acronyms, go to the Emoticons & Smileys page:

http://home.earthlink.net/~gripweeds/emoticon.htm

Emoticons

- Use these symbols to convey emotions in your messages. To see the faces in these symbols, turn the page to the right.

>:->	Angry	:-(	Sad
5:-)	Elvis	:-@	Scream
:-)	Happy	:-#	Secret (lips are sealed)
()	Hug	:P	Sticking Tongue Out
:-D	Joking	:-O	Surprised
:*	Kiss	:-J	Tongue in Cheek
:/)	Not Funny	;-)	Wink

Acronyms

- Listed below are some of the more-common acronyms, but new acronyms are always being created. Be sure to check online to see what's new.

ADN	Any day now	**GMTA**	Great minds think alike
ASAP	As soon as possible	**IAE**	In any event
B4N	Bye for now	**IMO**	In my opinion
BRB	Be right back	**IRL**	In real life
BTW	By the way	**JIC**	Just in case
DTRT	Do the right thing	**LOL**	Laugh out loud
F2F	Face to face	**ROTFL**	Rolling on the floor laughing
FAQ	Frequently asked questions	**RTM**	Read the manual
FWIW	For what it's worth	**TIA**	Thanks in advance
FYI	For your information	**WFM**	Works for me

Appendix C: Netiquette

Netiquette is the art of civilized communications between people on the Internet. Whenever you send an e-mail message, a chat room message, or a newsgroup message follow these guidelines.

A Few Tips

- Always include a subject in the message heading. This makes it easy for the recipient to organize messages in folders by topic and to find a message by browsing through message headers.

- Do not use capital letters. To the recipient, it feels like YOU ARE SHOUTING. Instead, enclose text that you want to emphasize with asterisks. For example: I *meant* Friday of *next* week.

- Be careful with the tone you use. With the absence of inflection, it is easy to send a message that can be misinterpreted by the recipient. Use emoticons to establish your intent. A smiley emoticon can make it clear to the recipient that you are really joking.

- Spell check your messages before you send them. They represent you.

- Do not send flame messages. These are obnoxious, offensive, or otherwise disturbing messages. If you send this type of message to a newsgroup, 30,000 people who read your flame will think less of you. If you receive flame mail, probably the best thing you can do is press the Delete button rather than the Reply button.

- Messages sent over the Internet are not private. Your message is in writing and nothing can prevent someone from forwarding it to anyone they please. Assume that anyone with a computer has the potential to read your message.

- If you send a long message, it is a good idea to tell the recipient at the beginning of the message so that they can decide if they would rather download it to read later.

- Never initiate or forward a chain letter. Some service providers will cancel your membership if you do so, as they are trying to protect their members from unwanted mail.

The Netiquette Home Page
http://www.albion.com/netiquette/index.html

- This page lists hyperlinks to pages on Netiquette contributed by Internet users. You will find interesting, amusing, and very important material in these sites.

Glossary

Listed below and on the following pages are terms that you may encounter on your Internet travels.

address book A place where frequently used e-mail addresses are stored.

anonymous FTP A special kind of FTP service that allows any user to log on. Anonymous FTP sites have a predefined user named "anonymous" that accepts any password.

Archie A database system of FTP resources. It helps you find files that exist anywhere on the Internet.

ARPAnet (Advanced Research Projects Administration Network)
Ancestor to the Internet: ARPAnet began in 1969 as a project developed by the US Department of Defense. Its initial purpose was to enable researchers and military personnel to communicate in the event of an emergency.

ASCII file (American Standard Code for Information Interchange) File containing ASCII-formatted text only; can be read by almost any computer or program in the world.

attachment File(s) or Web pages(s) enclosed with an e-mail message.

Base64 (MIME) encoding One of the encoding schemes, used in the MIME (Multipurpose Internet Mail Extensions) protocol.

binary file A file containing machine language (that is, ones and zeros) to indicate that the file is more than plain text. A binary file must be encoded (converted to ASCII format) before it can be passed through the e-mail system.

BinHex An encoding scheme for the Macintosh platform that allows a file to be read as text when passed through the e-mail system.

bookmark A browser feature that memorizes and stores the path to a certain Web site. Creating bookmarks enables a quick return to favorite sites.

Glossary

browser A graphic interface program that helps manage the process of locating information on the World Wide Web. Browser programs such as Netscape Navigator and Microsoft Internet Explorer provide simple searching techniques and create paths that can return you to sites you visited previously.

chat (Internet Relay Chat) A live "talk" session with other Internet or network users in which a conversation is exchanged back and forth.

client program A computer program designed to talk to a specific server program. The FTP client program is designed to ask for and use the FTP service offered by an FTP server program. Client programs usually run in your own computer, and talk to server programs in the computers it connects to.

client A computer that is signing onto another computer. The computer that is logging on acts as the client; the other computer acts as the server.

complex search Uses two or more words in a text string (and may also use operators that modify the search string) to search for matches in a search engine's catalog.

compressed file A file that has been made smaller (without lost data) by using a file compression program such as pkzip or StuffIt. Compressed files are easier to send across the Internet, as they take less time to upload and download.

copyright The legal right of ownership of published material. E-mail messages are covered by copyright laws. In most cases, the copyright owner is the writer of the message.

crawlers Another name for search engines.

directories Also referred to as folders. Directories are lists of files and other directories. They are used for organizing and storing computer files.

domain The portion of an Internet address that follows the @ symbol and identifies the computer you are logging onto.

downloading Copying files (e-mail, software, documents, etc.) from a remote computer to your own computer.

e-mail (electronic mail) A communication system for exchanging messages and attached files. E-mail can be sent to anyone in the world as long as both parties have access to the Internet and an Internet address to identify themselves.

encoding A method of converting a binary file to ASCII format for e-mail purposes. Common encoding schemes include Uuencoding and MIME (Base64) encoding.

fair use The right to use short quotes and excerpts from copyrighted material such as e-mail messages.

FAQ (Frequently Asked Questions document) A text document that contains a collection of frequently asked questions about a particular subject. FAQs on many subjects are commonly available on the Web.

file "File" is a general term usually used to describe a computer document. It may also be used to refer to more than one file, however, such as groups of documents, software, games, etc.

folders/ directories Folders, also referred to as directories, are organized storage areas for maintaining computer files. Like filing cabinets, they help you manage your documents and files.

font A typeface that contains particular style and size specifications.

freeware Software that can be used for free forever. No license is required and the software may be copied and distributed legally.

FTP (File Transfer Protocol) The method of remotely transferring files from one computer to another over a network (or across the Internet). It requires that both the client and server computers use special communication software to talk to one another.

FTP site An Internet site that uses File Transfer Protocol and enables files to be downloaded and/or uploaded. When you access an FTP site through a browser application, however, your log-in is considered "anonymous" and will not allow uploading.

FTP (File Transfer Protocol) A computer program used to move files from one computer to another. The FTP program usually comes in two parts: a server program that runs in the computers offering the FTP service, and a client program running in computers, like yours, that wish to use the service.

Gopher A menu system that allows you to search various sources available on the Internet. It is a browsing system that works much like a directory or folder. Each entry may contain files and/or more directories to dig through.

heading fields (headings) Individual fields, like To and From, in the header of an e-mail message.

hierarchically structured catalog A catalog of Web sites that is organized into a few major categories that have sub-categories under them. Each sub-category has additional sub-categories under it. The level of detail in this structure depends on the particular Web site.

home page A Web site's starting point. A home page is like a table of contents. It outlines what a particular site has to offer, and usually contains connecting links to other related areas of the Internet as well.

host A central computer that other computers log onto for the purpose of sharing and exchanging information.

hot lists Lists of Web sites that you have visited or "ear-marked" and wish to return to later. Your browser program will store the paths to those sites and generate a short-cut list for future reference.

HTML (HyperText Mark Up Language) The programming language used to create Web pages so that they can be viewed, read, and accessed from any computer running on any type of operating system.

HTTP (HyperText Transfer Protocol) The communication protocol that allows for Web pages to connect to one another, regardless of what type of operating system is used to display or access the files.

hypertext or hypermedia The system of developing clickable text and objects (pictures, sound, video, etc.) to create links to related documents or different sites on the Internet.

inbox Where incoming e-mail messages are stored and retrieved.

Information Superhighway Nickname for the Internet: a vast highway by which countless pieces of information are made available and exchanged back and forth among its many users.

Internet A world-wide computer network that connects several thousand businesses, schools, research foundations, individuals, and other networks. Anyone with access can log on, communicate via e-mail, and search for various types of information.

Internet address The user ID utilized by an individual or host computer on the Internet. An Internet address is usually associated with the ID used to send and receive e-mail. It consists of the user's ID followed by the domain.

Internet Protocol The method of communication which allows information to be exchanged across the Internet and across varying platforms that may be accessing or sending information.

ISP (Internet Service Providers) Private or public organizations that offer access to the Internet. Most charge a monthly or annual fee and generally offer such features as e-mail accounts, a pre-determined number of hours for Internet access time (or unlimited access for a higher rate), special interest groups, etc.

links Hypertext or hypermedia objects that, once selected, will connect you to related documents or other areas of interest.

login A process by which you gain access to a computer by giving it your username and password. If the computer doesn't recognize your login, access will be denied.

macro virus A virus written in the macro language of a particular program (such as Word) and contained in a program document. When the document is opened, the macro is executed, and the virus usually adds itself to other, similar documents. Macro virus can be only as destructive as the macro language allows.

message header The group of heading fields at the start of every e-mail program, used by the e-mail system to route and otherwise deal with your mail.

meta-tree structured catalog Another term for hierarchically structured catalog.

modem A piece of equipment (either internal or external) that allows a computer to connect to a phone line for the purpose of dialing into the Internet, another network, or an individual computer.

modem speed (baud rate) Indicates at what speed your computer will be able to communicate with a computer on the other end. The higher the rate, the quicker the response time for accessing files and Web pages, processing images, downloading software, etc.

multimedia The process of using various computer formats: pictures, text, sound, movies, etc.

multithread search engines Software that searches the Web sites of other search engines and gathers the results of these searches for your use.

netiquette (Network etiquette) The network equivalent of respectfulness and civility in dealing with people and organizations.

network A group of computers (two or more) that are connected to one another through various means, usually cable or dial-in connections.

newsgroup A bulletin board of news information. Users specify which news topic they are interested in, and subscribe to receive information on that topic.

newsreader A program that allows you to read and respond to Usenet newsgroups.

offline The process of performing certain tasks, such as preparing e-mail messages, prior to logging onto the Internet.

online The process of performing certain tasks, such as searching the Web or responding to e-mail, while actually logged onto the Internet.

online services Organizations that usually offer Internet access as well as other services, such as shareware, technical support, group discussions, and more. Most online services charge a monthly or annual fee.

operators Words or symbols that modify the search string instead of being part of it.

outbox Where offline e-mail messages are stored. The contents of an outbox are uploaded to the Internet once you log on and prompt your e-mail program to send them.

packet A body of information that is passed through the Internet. It contains the sender's and receiver's addresses and the item that is being sent. Internet Protocol is used to route and process the packet.

platform Refers to the type of computer and its corresponding operating system, such as PC, Macintosh, UNIX. The Internet is a multi-platform entity, meaning that all types of computers can access it.

POP (Post Office Protocol) The method used to transfer e-mail messages from your mail server to your system.

public domain freeware Software that can be used for free; usually the author is anonymous.

quote format A way of displaying text quoted from other e-mail messages, most frequently used in replies. Quoted text usually has a character like ">" at the start of each line. Some e-mail programs let you set the style of quoted material.

search engine A software program that goes out on the Web, seeks Web sites, and catalogs them – usually by downloading their home pages.

search sites Web sites that contain catalogs of Web resources that can be searched by headings, URLs, and key words.

self-extracting archive Macintosh-platform compressed file that does not require external software for decompression. These files usually end with an .sea extension.

self-extracting file PC-platform compressed file that does not require external software for decompression. These files usually end with an .exe extension.

server program A computer program that offers a service to other computer programs called client programs. The FTP server program offers the FTP service to FTP client programs. Server programs usually run in computers you will be connecting to.

server A computer that is accessed by other computers on a network. It usually shares files with or provides other services to the client computers that log onto it.

shareware Computer programs, utilities and other items (fonts, games, etc.) that can be downloaded or distributed free of charge, but with the understanding that if you wish to continue using it, you will send the suggested fee to the developer.

signature A few lines of text automatically appended to the body of an e-mail message. Signatures usually include the sender's address plus other information.

simple search Uses a text string, usually a single word, to search for matches in a search engine's catalog.

.sit file A Macintosh file compressed by using a compression application called StuffIt.

SLIP (Serial Line Internet Protocol) Software that allows for a direct serial connection to the Internet. SLIP allows your computer to become part of the Internet – not just a terminal accessing the Internet. If your computer is set up with SLIP, you can Telnet or FTP other computers directly without having to go through an Internet provider.

SMTP (Simple Mail Transfer Protocol) The method used to transfer e-mail messages between servers and from your system to your mail server.

spiders Another name for search engines.

standalone FTP client program A standalone computer program designed to talk to an FTP server program running at a remote computer site that offers FTP services. The FTP client program can ask for the files you want and send files you wish to deliver. The client program runs in your computer; the server program runs at the site.

start page The opening page within a browser application. This is the page from which all other Web site links are built. A browser's start page is its home page by default, but you can customize your browser to begin with any Web site as your start page.

subject-structured catalog A catalog organized under a few broad subject headings. The number and names of these headings depend on the Web site.

surfing the Internet Exploring various World Wide Web sites and links to search for information on the Internet. Using FTP, WAIS, and Gopher servers can further assist in the surfing/searching process – as can a good Internet browser.

TCP/IP (Transmission Control Protocol/ Internet Protocol) The communication system that is used between networks on the Internet. It checks to make sure that information is being correctly sent and received from one computer to another.

Telnet A program that allows one computer to log on to another host computer. This process allows you to use any of the features available on the host computer, including sharing data and software, participating in interactive discussions, etc.

text format file Same as the ASCII format file: a document that has been formatted to be read by almost any computer or program in the world.

text string A string of ASCII characters. The text string may or may not contain operators.

threaded messages Messages grouped so that replies to a message are grouped with the original message. When threaded messages are sorted, threads are kept together.

uploading The process of copying computer files (e-mail, software, documents, etc.) from one's own computer to a remote computer.

URL (Uniform Resource Locator) A locator command used only within the World Wide Web system to create or hunt for linked sites. It operates and looks much like an Internet Address.

Usenet A world-wide discussion system, operating on linked Usenet servers, consisting of a set of newsgroups where articles or messages are posted covering a variety of subjects and interests. You can use your browser or a newsreader program to access the newsgroups available from your Internet provider's Usenet server.

UUencoding One of the encoding schemes, short for UNIX-to-UNIX encoding. UUencoding is common on all platforms, not just UNIX.

virus A small, usually destructive computer program that hides inside innocent-looking programs. Once the virus is executed, it attaches itself to other programs. When triggered, often by the occurrence of a date or time on the computer's internal clock/calendar, it executes a nuisance or damaging function, such as printing a message or reformatting your hard disk.

WAIS (Wide Area Information Servers) A system that allows for searches for information based on actual contents of files, not just file titles.

Web robots Software which automatically searches the Web for new sites.

Web Site A location on the Internet that represents a particular company, organization, topic, etc. It normally contains links to more information within a site, as well as suggested links to related sites on the Internet.

World Wide Web (WWW) An easy-to-use system for finding information on the Internet through the use of hypertext or hypermedia linking. Hypertext and hypermedia consist of text and graphic objects that, when you click on them, automatically link you to different areas of a site or to related Internet sites.

zip file PC file compressed with pkzip. Zipped files usually need to be unzipped with pkunzip before they can be used.

Index

Index